HE LOVED ME SOME DAYS
I'M SURE HE DID

99 essays on growth through loss

By Charlotte Eriksson
The Glass Child

He loved me some days. I'm sure he did.

99 essays on growth through loss

———————

Cover artwork by Ivana Lena Besevic

DISCOGRAPHY
Charlotte Eriksson EP, *2011*
This Is How Ghosts Are Made EP, *2011*
Songs of An Insomniac EP, *2011*
I'd Like To Remain A Mystery, LP *2013*
Empty Roads & Broken Bottles: in search for The Great Perhaps, book 2013
Love Always, Your Tragedy EP, 2013
I Must Be Gone and Live or Stay and Die, LP 2014
Another Vagabond Lost To Love, book 2015
You're Doing Just Fine, book 2015
Under Northern Skies, *LP* 2016
This Silence Now EP, 2017
Coming Home EP, 2017
Songs That Shaped Me, EP 2018
Everything Changed When I Forgave Myself, book 2018
Feeling Everything, Holding on to Nothing, LP 2021
He loved me some days. I'm sure he did, book 2021

Someone you can't live without

I am clumsy, drop glasses and get drunk on Monday afternoons. I read Seneca and can recite Shakespeare by heart,

but I mess up the laundry, don't answer my phone and blame the world when something goes wrong. I think I have a dream, but most days I'm still sleeping.

The grass is cut. The air smells like strawberries. Today I finished four books and cleaned out my drawers.

Do you believe in a God? Can I tell you about Icarus? How he flew too close to the sun?

I want to make coming home your favorite part of the day. I want to leave small words lingering in your mind, on nights when you're far away and can't sleep. I want to make everything around us beautiful. Make small things mean a little more. Make you feel a little more. A little better, a little lighter.

The coffee is warm, this cup is yours. I want to be someone you can't live without.

I want to be someone you can't live without.

Preface

I want you to read this book not with your eyes or with your education or with a clock ticking behind you. I want you to read it slowly but also fast, like a breath, in your own rhythm, and when a line stands out to you, like it does sometimes, I want you to stop and take a breath and read it again. Maybe scribble it in a notebook, or on your phone, or in your palm, because take my word for it: the older you get, the harder it is to read something that truly touches you. You know, something that grips you and makes you feel like the sky is a little closer and the world a little further away and it's just you and the sky and this author. Suddenly the universe is a little bit more holy.

Yeah, that thing, it doesn't happen as often when you're no longer young and worried and sad but also excited and hungry for salvation or ecstasy. You're grounded now. You think twice before letting anything get to you. You've been burnt and bent a few times so your skin is thicker. You no longer stay up watching the moon because you have work to do in the morning and you simply get on with things.

This book is really not about anything at all. It's not profound or coherent or edited. Just so you know.

I feel whole when I write. I feel like a fraud when I don't write. I don't really feel like I have anything incredible to tell. But I also don't think I do not have anything incredible to tell. So I'll just write, I thought, and see what happens. I started writing every day for 30 days and 30 days turned into 60 and then I finished a book and then I wrote for 60 more days and now I'm not sure what day I'm on but I write and it makes me feel whole and like I'm not a fraud and so I will keep writing.

I write this for you. Meaning you as a friend. I address you, because I am too old to write for myself or people who are no longer in my life.

And by 'too old' I mean my age counted out in the nights when I felt finished. Those were many but they don't come as often anymore, and when they do come, I know I'll get through them now.

I asked him why he's so scared to commit and he said he's not scared to commit, he's just not in the mood to commit to me because he's committed to himself, and I knew in that instant I wanted him more than I've ever wanted anything. I wanted to be with him, but I also wanted to be him, replace myself with him and find a girl like me who look at me like I looked at him when he said that.

Am I committed to myself? Yes, but I let myself down sometimes, in different ways. But it will change now. I can count on myself now, to do what I say I will do. Geez, I hate people who only talk talk talk but then act in the opposite direction and it's just tiring. I used to see those people and say, "I'm done with boys, I want a man!" But I am just a girl and I'd like to be a woman. True to her words. Committed to herself, strong and soft but always committed to herself.

Okay, this will all be fragmented because I have so much to say but not one BIG thing to say, just many small things, so I will let it all flow through me and you catch what you can and let go of what you can't, okay?

I realize I've never told you how I write, or how I meditate, or how I pray, or what I pray to
and I don't think I ever told you about the night I fell down the ladder by the fire escape
because I was drunk and sad after a fight with my mum, or my ex-boyfriend, I can't remember,
but I fell down the ladder because I was drunk and sad and I injured my knee a little and when my ex-boyfriend asked about it I thought

about using it against him, like blaming him for making me climb up the ladder so he would feel guilty and then love me a little more.

But that's not how love works. I know that now but I didn't back then.

Anyway, I don't think you knew this about me.

But you do know my age and where I'm from and maybe where I go for drinks on Thursday evenings in October, in Berlin where I live now. Quite a few people know the sound I make the second I fall asleep because I didn't have a home for so very long, because I was stubborn and just wanted to be a songwriter. Though I didn't make any money so I slept on my friends' couches or rugs or in their bathtubs or whatever they offered me and I was fine with that, for a few years.

But I never told you about the trip to Portugal 3 years ago when I read Fernando Pessoa at 1 a.m. outside a small family-run restaurant by the harbor. If I close my eyes I can still smell the salt water and the fish, some sort of cleaning powder scent from the kitchen, can still feel the heat, a soft wind and me sitting with wide open eyes on my own at 1 a.m. writing what I thought was profound and excellent. I felt like a writer then. I was not a girlfriend or a daughter or a songwriter who never got signed—I was a writer in the truest sense and I lived in my own flames.

Yes, I do pray—I didn't tell you? I pray to the sky and the moon and the Earth, saying: "Thank you for protecting me. Thank you, Earth, for supporting me and thank you, sky, for looking over me." I close my eyes and feel the sky above and the earth beneath and then I take a deep breath and feel safe enough to fall asleep.

He says he's in love with me but he does not know that I pray or meditate, where I go to write and how I write and he does not know that I cry every midnight because I'm simply tired, even if I'm already in bed trying to sleep, next to him.

He compliments my intellect but he does not ask how I learn or who I learn from. He wants to hear me sing but he wouldn't hear what I was singing about so I mumble an excuse and walk away.

But he's committed to himself and I like that. I like that so much I forget about everything else. Am I committed to myself? I'm committed to my ideas. I'm committed to my work. That's practically me, right? My ideas and my work. Maybe I have some kindness somewhere too but I'm not sure it shows.

I drank a lot when I wrote my other books. Actually, I drank a lot when I wrote this book too because I wrote this a while ago but we'll get to that in a few paragraphs.

I didn't know I was writing books though, and I didn't know I was drinking a lot because I also wasn't eating, anything at all, really, but I didn't see it as a problem because I just wanted to write. I would like to believe you can write from a place of logic and calm but I'm also grateful some people get drunk or high or whatever you prefer and write not from logic but from a raw, strange, in-between state of mind where everything is more real and not so real at the same time because the writings are magical. I think?

Sometimes I wish I was young enough again to not care about tomorrow. I didn't back then but now I do.

Okay, I'll stop with the small talk. I'll get to it now. If you were sitting in front of me now, I would strum my fingers on the table and flick my eyes and probably find a joke to crack before you'd say, "Just get to it already" and I would act like I just forgot, like, "Oh right! Of course, so…" and then ask for another drink. Which I practically just did in writing but here it goes:

This book is a journal of poems and prose and daily scribblings I wrote while being in a long relationship that pulled me over and buried me a little and then forced me to start anew with absolutely everything. It was the longest relationship I've ever been in. Also the saddest one. Also the happiest. Also the one that taught me more than anything else has ever taught me. About myself and other people and everything in between. At first I thought, *This is it.* But you always do, right? You have to, otherwise you don't even start.

I started writing this book a year in when I had just given up on my own story and path and plans to instead move to his city. I thought the move would make things easier for myself, but I cursed it and started a journal I called *Lonely in Love.* Still I thought he was "the one"! Can you believe that??! As I sit here older, now, healed and redesigned, I think of that girl and still feel the enormous amount of love she carried for this one person but she did not know how to do it. How to love. That's fucking hard, you know, it's not something you're just born with. How do you express that sort of love? That love that makes you feel happy and nauseous all at once. How do you show it and save it? care for it and nurture it? That girl I was didn't know so she ruined it. Not by herself, of course, there are always two people ruining love together, but this girl did her part, for sure.

She wanted so much. She wanted the world, but she could not conquer it so she found a boy she thought was the world and maybe he could invite her into it. Maybe he could be her world.
It turns out you can't make the world out of a human and you can't move in and you can't expect him to make *you* his whole world—but how would you know that when you've never tried before? How can you know when there is no course in how to love or how not to lose yourself or how to simply be happy and fine and healed and loved all at once?

This is not a book about love and how to make it last, but isn't everything about love and how to make it last? I think I could write a book about pets or politics or museums and it would still be about love and how to make it last because isn't that the whole thing of absolutely everything: love and how to make it last?

I didn't love my life but now I do. I'm sure I will fall out of love with it again at some point but I'm confident I will go to therapy and work it out and fall back in love with it.

I didn't love my body and my mind and my ways of being but now I do. Okay, not every day but 5 out of 7, for sure. I'm lying but I know I can get there if I keep working on it.

I didn't love people because I felt lonely and no one made me unlonely and I blamed them. But now I realize the loneliness is an inside job. I can love them or not love them independent of their love for me, but the loneliness is dependent on not loving very many things. So now I try to love a lot.

That's a truth, you know, you should write that down: loneliness is dependent on not loving very many things or people so you should try to love as many things and people as you possibly can. Loneliness can't survive when there is too much love around.

Did you write that down?

Okay, back to the book: This is a book that I started writing in April 2014. That's when this all started, a dark circle that led to a really dark abyss and then a rebirth, but I'm getting ahead of myself. I finished this book in April 2020, because that's when I let this all go and turned around and started a new chapter, truly. And the whole time during those years I hid this book in a folder on my computer thinking I could never publish this because it would hurt him and ruin us and I would never do that, but see now I think I would. Nah, I take that back, but things are different now. It really is true, you know, that time heals all wounds. I didn't believe it just a year ago. I was still sad and heartbroken, desperately trying to get him back. But it only took one night with someone new who looked at me like I was pretty special to make me realise I had made a world out of one single person and that's pretty limiting because, you know, the world is pretty limitless. There are people out there who will love you like you love them and all that jazz, but that's a different book.

I also believe in living life in cycles. It takes 7 years for your body to replace every single cell, meaning every 7th year you are a completely different physical person. I think your mind and circumstances should follow suit. I mean, you can't replace your entire physical body and expect the life that the previous body lived in to still fit. You have a new body so you must find a new life to inhabit with new people, maybe, and so you must go on. But that is also another book, and I don't want to make this preface too long.

So, this is a story about young love. The kind of young love that makes you want to rip your heart out because you're old enough to know that you truly deeply love this person but you're still young enough to not know how to let yourself be loved and love in the right way and ... you know ... communicate.
This is a book about how it really is possible to grow through heartbreak. Enter like a child and exit like an adult. Really, truly feeling it.

I wrote 207 songs during the years this love encompassed, which might not sound like a lot but it is a lot, trust me. 12 of those songs made it onto an album called *feeling everything, holding on to nothing*. This book and that album go hand in hand. They belong together.

It takes so long to learn how to love but I think it starts with messing it up a few times. Maybe next time I'll get it right.

No matter what, he loved me some days. I'm sure he did. At least now I love myself, and I don't think I would if he still loved me.

I don't think I would love myself if I still loved him.

The lonely winter

Prague, 2014

That was the winter of learning empty space. Learning a tight pressure around my chest, waiting to explode and break out. But no matter how far you travel or how long you wander, how cold it grows or how drunk you get, the tight pressure just stays in there. You meditate, pray, fast, and run, thinking it's some kind of detoxification process. A stone of toxic memories from all things yesterday and you just need to release it, let go and clean yourself pure. But the stone stays in there. A big, black stone of heaviness. Sadness. The snow fell. The streets turned white. People walked quietly hand in hand with baskets of treats from the Christmas market. The 25th arrived and I woke in a hostile hotel in the old part of town. The older gentleman in the reception played Spanish Christmas music as I said good morning and made my way to the streets. It was a beautiful morning. Snow had fallen again during the night and the town was dressed in a gentle blanket of white powder.

I had no plan. Just another Christmas of trying to make it right, like I've done so many times these years. Organizing myself and my mind, my things and plans, what to do and where to go, just trying to keep on top of it; putting in the good hours. One good day, one good piece of writing, one good song. That's all.

I passed the bridge that I recalled falling in love with the first time I saw it. I had read about it in so many poems, in so many novels with great destinies. It was the first time architecture had made me spellbound. That first time I walked around in feverish happiness, feeling free once again with endless views.

It had been a cold year in Berlin. My only goal was to survive and get through, build myself up again, inside out. I needed a stronger foundation. A solid base to stand on, to not fall down, like I'd done so many times before. I needed a better base. So I got through and the holidays came and went. Christmas, New Year, birthdays, and spring, and I kept wandering those streets still trying not to rush my direction. I trusted my instinct to find a pace and a place to go from here but for now, I just needed to walk.

Anyway, it's Christmas again and I'm walking lonely in Prague, escaping the vast existence I've put myself in. I love it still. The freedom to stretch my legs, read as I please, and work on my novel (a dream can get you far). There is time for intellectual growth, which feels like salvation these days. My coffee shop is open as usual. The man behind the bar nods and gives me a soft smile, an acknowledgement of us both spending Christmas morning by ourselves in small coffee shops.

I curse my ways and seek escapes, but I love it still—I wouldn't change a thing. I love knowing that nothing is permanent, only here for the moment. My life is simple but decadent, filled with smoke and dark places, though my sky is always blue. It's a contradiction I can't figure out and don't want to because I never know who I'll be when I wake up, where I'll wake up or if I'll feel the urge to run away and start anew. I observe myself like in a movie and I'm the most fascinating character I'll never fully figure out. Like a child, never knowing what the next move will be.

I'll find my group one day. Friends I belong with, a city, a community, a place to get all those ideas out and let them be heard and appreciated. I'll be something one day. I know I will. For now, I'm walking lonely in Prague at Christmas, feeling like the happiest, most unknown girl in the world.

LOVE IS ALWAYS NEW

It starts like this

It's the smell of him in the bathroom, all I need to get ready for the day. Watching him get dressed, and the sounds in the kitchen; a slow hum of a song and his movements, picking things to eat. The way I could observe him, for hours, just go on with his day—or as he sleeps —breathing in and out, in and out, the hymn that sings me to peace. I know the world is still out there and I know I'm not yet friendly to its pace, but as long as I know him with me, here, there, somewhere —us—I know I have a chance.

Journal I

Hamburg, 2015

August. Summer. I got the key to my new home. A small room in the basement of a mansion, a rich lady practicing the violin to a metronome until midnight every night. I have a bed, a big white desk and a place for my books, which is all I'm looking for—all I need. I put my microphone up, my guitar, three notebooks in different sizes, and the candle I've kept in my rucksack from Edinburgh, to Bristol, to Berlin, Prague, Hamburg … thinking the moment is never special enough to light it, but now it will be.

I said goodbye to Berlin after two years of aimless wandering, drinking, watching, and missing the last bus home. The drunken youth served me well in that city and I never felt alone even though I was, always someone being interesting or interested enough for another drink, another time, another night. Hamburg is quiet. Clean. Families walking hand in hand on Sunday mornings and I hear German for the first time since I moved to Germany. In Berlin I spent my mornings drifting from coffee shop to coffee shop, writing my novel, writing my record, writing whatever I could write, and I loved it. No one questioned my intentions and I was left alone. Here the owners of the coffee shops look at me in a foreign way, like they don't really know why I'm here. "Can I come in? Sorry to interrupt?"
I place myself in the corner of a busy cafe a few streets from my new home. A stressed-out woman hands me the menu with a phrase in German I don't understand yet but I smile, hoping I don't have to say more than necessary.

I know one person in this town and that's why I moved here. I'm too stubborn, holding on to French novels, believing love can save us all, but I know I will have to save myself. I have my work, I have my music, and I like the challenge of trying to feel at home anywhere, even in a city where I don't understand people or their ways. or can be understood, and I like the idea of closing the door. Rimbaud wrote:

"The first task of a man who wants to be a poet is to study his own self-awareness, in its entirety; he seeks out his soul, he inspects it, he tests it, he learns it. […] I say that one must be a Seer, make oneself a Visionary.

The Poet makes himself a seer by a long, prodigious, and rational disorganization of all the senses. All the forms of love, of suffering, of madness; he searches himself."

I have a romanticized idea about dedicating myself to my work, to live and die for it and let nothing else interrupt. To live and learn all there is to live and learn in order to be a great writer, a great artist: all I came here to be.

I bought a small lamp for my desk, candles, dark curtains to keep the light out and cheap wine from Italy because the person I moved here for is from Italy so I'm trying to learn his ways.

The winter came fast and I spent endless nights and early mornings in my basement. I read hundreds of novels, studied them like a scholar. I wrote about all things past, all things now and all things future. Studied songs and instruments, arrangements and productions, and I dedicated myself to my work as best I could. Hamburg was right outside my window—a quiet street, though still a part of it—but I stayed in my basement, letting nothing disturb me.

My person was lovely at times, angry at others, mostly tired from living and succeeding—I was not a part of it. The French novel I dreamt of stayed in my notebooks and my person was too tired to love.

This is a story about love and how not to love and sometimes exactly how to love, but mostly how to love something other than your love for another person because in the end, you have to save yourself. You must place that love in something more solid than a fleeting person because when it's gone you have to have love left for your own life.

From loneliness to love

How do you move from loneliness to love?

How do you embrace this space all around, this emptiness that strangles and suffocates? That freedom that once captivated you. You dreamt of complete detachment, being able to roam the world, no more commitments, no more tasks to do. No one would chain you in. And now you live in this vast freedom and you can't find your way out. You just want to go inside somewhere. Sit down by a table. Have dinner with people who care about you. You just want to listen to some old man's tale by the fireplace, hold someone's hand, fall asleep next to someone who would notice if you went missing.

How do you move from loneliness to love?

This vast freedom around me. I can't hold it. I can't escape it. I can't live in it.

How do I fill it with love and life? It's so quiet. It's so grey. Like a thick winter fog all around me every morning as I start my day. That kind of morning fog that's peaceful and beautiful, reflecting clarity and fresh air. But it's all around and it doesn't clear up.

I make coffee. I sit down to write. The fog starts where my breath ends. I see nothing other than my own sphere for the moment. I see my own hands, I hear my own voice. But I see no people, I see no landscape. I close my eyes and envision my future but I open my eyes again and all I see is my own life moving like a bubble inside this thick greyness. Sometimes I go crazy and think I'm all alone in the world. I forget there are people outside of that fog, in between me and the world.

Sometimes I like it here. In the mist. I live my own life undisturbed. Nothing can touch me. I study, I read, I learn, I write. I go for walks and enjoy the silence. I enjoy the stillness. I have lists of things I want to master. Maybe one day I'll be really great at something.

Then it gets late and I'm so tired but it takes me five hours to lie down in my bed, on my own. Draw the curtains over a world I'm not part of. Turn out the lights. Close my eyes. Invite the thoughts, the memories, the nostalgia.

How do you move from loneliness to love?

The Notebook

He gave me a notebook made of real, brown leather, and we are not people who buy things
or give things
as a means of love
but he gave me a notebook to keep my thoughts in
and songs in
because he knows I collect them like treasures and he liked giving them to me.

I don't often value material belongings and often they lie like burdens in my chest, knowing I have to give something back, now, but this notebook was different because he didn't need to give me anything. He did it simply because he wanted to. "I thought of you."

I went home and as the darkness spread I opened the first page, pen in hand, candles lit, and said to myself, *This can be my little book of love! I will fill it with beautiful thoughts and lines and words and each page will be marked with his name.*

But as I set pen to paper my mind went blank. Not a word within reach, all escaped and
what do you mean *write about love*? no no no, you can't do that, you are not like that, don't live like that.

And I saw them all shaking their heads, saying, "She's lost her uniqueness, her talent"
"Just another book of love"
because I used to write about other things that matter. Like life, youth, shame, and sorrow
and I still do and still feel those things
but did you know I cured my own anxiety by reading philosophy? Did you know I'm off medication and live on plant-based food? I run and meditate and try to keep in touch? Did you know I poured the booze down the drain because I tried to blur out myself until I almost

disappeared? Drowned my regrets in stronger liquids and never enough food and I desired to be art in all kinds of ways.
I just wanted to be beautiful.

So I could write about these things that matter and always will,
but I could also write about love. How a hand can silence thousands of voices and how someone's smell can make you feel at home even though you're a million miles away from home
and have you ever hurt someone you love? Because you're angry. Because you're disappointed and sad and you just really wanted to love and be loved in return,
but life got in the way and you both said things that should never be said and you're angry but don't know how to. Because you still feel this strange love for him, but you're also fucking angry and you want to hit him, but then hug him because hurting him is hurting yourself, and then hit him again because you're angry! So you fall on your knees because you're hopeless to yourself and your own emotions
and that's love, my friend.

Never did I know that learning how to live with someone else could solve the "self" so elegantly.
I could write about sorrow and struggle, youth and regrets, but for now, I'd rather write about love. A little while, a long while, as long as I can.

The first page
of my little book of love.

Cure for Loneliness

I have found no other cure for loneliness than to befriend it. To sit with it. Feel it. Learn it. Every vibration and every ache. I tried to drink it away. I tried to smoke it away. I ran for miles and sang and cursed,
but there is no other cure for loneliness than to befriend it.

I live here now and this is my life. This is my bed; these are my shoes. That's my key and this is my street. That's where I buy coffee on Monday morning and that's where I go to write on dark nights in November.
I live here now.
That's the bench where I sat all night through August, when it was still warm and bright, no worries too cold to carry. These are my secrets and that is my door; you're welcome any time, I will never say no.

There is no other cure for loneliness than to befriend it. To sit with it. Feel it. Learn it. Every vibration and every ache. Embrace it, even.
You can't run away from being lonely, you can only learn to walk with it.

Brevity

He is sewing stitches over my chest. Piecing me back together day by day, rolling his fingers over my forehead.

I took a lighter and gathered all my notebooks, for they are messy and disconnected
but he is not, so neither will I be
anymore. desperate for a new start.
blank pages
to write better rhymes,
connected lines,
and now I can. I am facing my own reflection. How I walk, how I look, how I appear
and he's teaching me openness, how to simply speak. He's showing me how to keep in touch. To keep saying "good morning" and "I miss you" and things like figuring it out. Not giving up. Not just
leaving
and I thought that I was practicing essentialism
but I'm learning that elimination of the essentials is not a minimalist lifestyle worthy of honors
because it's simply lazy and cowardly
and sometimes the brave thing is not to go on by yourself
but to simply
not
go on by yourself
and I am learning to be brave.

I want to learn how to be brave.

Journal II

How do you know that someone loves you? How can you tell? I'm exciting at times, wild and free, but he's mostly bored. I can't excite him.

Every night I walk for 45 minutes to get to his house, thinking it's a nice act of love, showing I care: I'm willing to walk the miles. I imagine him opening the door, greeting me with a kiss and a smile, looking at me a little too long as you do when you think that person in front of you is wonderful. I dream about him looking at me like maybe I'm special, not just a face in the crowd, and I dream of him having made an effort. Dressed up for me, with one special rose bought that day from a florist, and I dream of him saying, "Happy birthday, I'm taking you out for dinner, your favorite restaurant and your favorite wine."

I smile all the way there, walking faster with my daydream and I imagine us happy, loving, being nice and I dream of myself making art and all things lovely and finally feeling at home. I've lived with a quiet ache in my heart lately, feeling slightly off, in this place, in this town, but I know if I can just go home to love, to him, to someone who looks at me like maybe I'm special ... then I could feel at home here, or anywhere. Together we will be fine.

I get there and it's dark. I ring the doorbell, he leaves the door open and I take my shoes off. "Hello?"

He has made dinner for himself, is eating in the kitchen. He says hi and tells me he's tired. He's got his pajamas on, ready to sleep, needs to shower, do laundry, answer emails. He's not up for a drink at the pub and I drink too much anyway, he tells me. I nod and smile, thinking he really is just tired.

I fall asleep on the right side of the bed, him turned to the other, his back towards me like a wall separating us. The cars drive by outside leaving flickers on the wall, one by one. I count them, wondering where they're going. Home to someone they love? Away to new adventures? A TV is humming from the flat above and someone's laughing next door.

How did I get here? How did I make this my home? I fall asleep next to the person I love more than anything, feeling like the loneliest girl in the world.

I learned how to cry without making a sound.

Clouds, clouds

One second you're thinking of leaving, one-way tickets and googling words in French. The other you're at IKEA buying more belongings, painting the walls, weighing you down with shallow commitments, one day to be burnt up.

It's always raining in this town, even when it's sunny it's raining and the rain is inhabiting my mind and brain and mood and heart and I'm growing smaller again.

I'm reading hymns and mantras, telling me to still my own storms and that no travel is needed if you can find satellites in your own heart. But it's always raining in this town, inhabiting my mind.

Clouds, clouds, always bright above the clouds.

Lessons in Love Nr. 1

This is not an educational book about love and how to make it last but loving someone and losing that someone is always an education in love and how to make it last. So we must take every opportunity we can to study and not repeat, okay?

I want to study younger me making all those mistakes, just meaning well but look at the mess she's making:

1. She tried to make a home out of a human, but you cannot make a home out of a human. You must build your home in small moments of belonging, and then little by little learn to feel belonged to yourself no matter where in the world you are or who you're with. So that you can feel at home in your own life, no matter where it might take you.

2. She woke up each morning hoping her person would love her and take her on adventures, but she had no agenda to love herself or create adventure. She wanted him to make her life exciting, but she was not exciting.

3. She wanted to be inspired but did not inspire because she put her life on hold, waiting for someone else to come home and have more time for her.

Let's start with those mistakes and let's not repeat them, okay?

Losing touch

I never write anymore.
I don't write.

I used to live in the ecstasy of hurt and pain, the longing for something far, far away and I was all in the middle of it. I was in so much pain. Such tremendous hurt and I did not know what to do with it. How to live with it or how to live without it and I wanted so much but had no reach to get there and
i wanted to be loved and love and still couldn't care less
and all I wanted was to feel myself. Here, okay?? are you okay? See, that's your heart, beating beating beating. It'll all be fine.
I lost people I loved and left people I loved and I had innocent girls writing letters about hospitals and needles and I wanted to help, wanted to make this a better place, a little softer place.
I lived right in the middle of all this.
Of hurt and pain and glorious sparks of nostalgia for brighter days and I believed in so much but had so little to give, so much left to throw off, and I lived right in the middle of all this. Burning hard and strong and bright and wrong
and I wrote it all down, hoping it would make things clearer.
I put my desk in the corner of my room that winter because the window distracted me with too much to see and I needed to write. I put my desk in the corner that winter and wrote day and night, through and through and I had so much to tell, so much to share.

xx   x

I don't write here. My desk is placed in the middle of the room and it's clean and bright, candles and flowers and books neatly on their shelves.

No one says my name anymore. In that way I used to love so much. Oh how I loved it, hearing my name, like the beginning of a sentence, someone wanting to share something with me, for real! Someone being excited and enthusiastic to share something of importance or non-importance but nonetheless, they wanted to share it, with me!
I used to imagine my name being the beginning of the most wonderful stories of lofty days, and I never had enough, could listen to people tell me things day in and night out but
no one says my name here. I don't hear my name anymore.

I walked the streets of those towns that year. Those streets, those years. of Gothenburg, of London,
of Brighton of Bristol of Prague of Edinburgh of Berlin…
But there are no streets to be walked here. There are no streets in this town.

I don't walk the streets, in any town, and my name is not said and I never write anymore. At night I dream of intense colors and intense pain and intense feelings or experiences. I wake up exhausted from all this non-living and I go on with my day.

I can't remember the sound of my name.
I don't write anymore.

Welcome home

You're thinking, maybe it would be easier to let it slip
let it go
say "I give up" one last time and give him a sad smile.
You're thinking
it shouldn't be this hard,
shouldn't be this dark,
thinking
love could flow easily with no holding back
and you've seen others find their match and build something great
together,
of each other,
like two halves fitting perfectly and now they achieve great things
one by one, always together, and it seems grand.
But you love him. Love him like a black stone in your chest you
couldn't live without because it fits in there. Makes you who you are
and the thought of him gone—no more—makes your chest tighten
up and
maybe this is your fairy tale. Maybe this is your castle.

You could get it all on a shiny piece of glass with wooden stools and a
never-ending blooming garden
but that's not yours. This is yours. The cracks and the faults,
the ugly words in the winter
walking home alone and angry
but falling asleep thinking you love him.
This is your fairy tale.
The quiet in the hallway, wishing for him to turn around, tell you to
stay, tell you to please don't go I need you
like you need me
and maybe it's not a Jane Austen novel but this is *your* novel and
your castle

and you can run from it your whole life but this is here
in front of you.
Maybe nurture it?
Maybe close the world off and look at him for an hour
or two.
This is your fairy tale.
It ain't perfect and it ain't honey-sweet with roses on the bed.
It's real and raw and ugly at times, but this is *your* love.
Don't throw it away searching for someone else's love. Don't be greedy. Instead, shelter it. Protect it. Capture every second of easy, pull through every storm of hardship. And when you can, look at him, lying next to you, trusting you not to harm him. Trusting you not to go.
Be someone's someone.
Be that someone for him.

That's your fairy tale. This is your castle.
Now move in. Build a home. Build a house. Build safety around things you love.
It's yours if you make it so.

Welcome home, it will all be fine.

Nothing new to say

So we live now, on memories remembered well. Like soft kisses, a
midsummer midnight
when we were younger, lighter, not yet habitual lovers,
saying goodnight from separate sides of the bed. The roads are still
out there, being washed clean every morning
for people like you,
like me,
and they lead everywhere, anywhere, nowhere at all.
But I make the bed each day here, wash the dishes and pay my dues.
Passing the train station on my way to the store, the gym, the chores
of every day
like every other
and everything is in order.
Everything is in order now.

I have nothing to write home about
anymore.
I have nothing new to say.

Music for a living

People play music for a living here and I'm still trying to figure out how to live the other way around.

I took a walk to the wrong side of town last night, when things got quiet, and I walked past houses with well-shaped bushes and manicured trees. The pavement is whole here. No cracks or worn-out heels, no people sleeping on the concrete.

I want to write words with other sounds like
wouahi liba thkaaa
that don't make sense 'cause it speaks loud now
and I write my songs but then need to convince myself not to throw myself out of the nearest window
right after
because who am I writing for and why and no one will hear it, ever, anyway
and people run their races here. It's all about the scale, the ladder, the road to the top
and they're having their ways. Wages and stages and well-adapted travels
as I mention thoughts about "why" and "who" and "please"
but people run their races here. Chasing wages and larger stages
while I'm walking lonely in yet another city, with yet another heavy tale to tell
with no one to listen
and I think I've switched the wall for my ladder too many times
for people have gone and moved on, while I'm left alone on the ground, still trying to find my own
time,
peace
of

mind,
and I'm doing alright.
They say I'm doing alright.

Larry Rivers, the great painter, said: "It's life we're interested in, not art," and I think somewhere maybe I focused too hard on the top of the finger, when I really wanted to see where it was pointing. What's art without life? (What's life without art?)

I am good with the questions. I pour them over everyone I meet and people run the other way because I'm throwing thoughts and critique and want people to think, loud, and let me hear—let me in (I am always on the outside). Why do you do what you do? Who are you trying to impress? Do you ever feel shame? Do you tell jokes to make people laugh or to make people think you're funny?

What does love mean to you, and do you think you can keep it?

What about loneliness?

People write music for a living here.
I only wanted to live to get to write music.

Journal III

I'm learning the important phase of staying in one place. Of withdrawing from the public and approval of the crowd. I have slowly entered a phase of inward work. Of divine, way more important activities.

I'm reading Seneca's letters and he's talking about the deeper value in one interaction with one person, eye to eye, rather than preaching empty words to please the whole audience. Therefore I am closing the door to write words aimed at one person: my younger self, my older self, the me in all its shapes. And if my calculations and beliefs are right, these words will then reach deeper into the right many. Not the whole crowd, but the right ones.

Fiction

Who is it about?
he asked
knowing the name
which was not his.

This is how I do it:
I invent a house; dark, no furniture or neighbors around. I need
someone in there; I invent a man. A kind man with too much heart. I
place him on the doorstep, not knowing how to enter this room, now,
where he's supposed to live.
I need a hobby, a job, he might have been a teacher once, because he
likes kids and the sound of laughter and he was happy with that.
I need a history, of leaving or arriving, and I will place him with a
woman who turned around 'cause she got bored. Too young for
stillness and the man who never changed and now I need an ending
but endings are rare
and I never write them
only leave
so what do I have?
I have a man, a history, a house with no story
and I can go wherever I want from here.

I invent neighbors and children, a family and hobbies and the man is
running everywhere and nowhere and I can write his future or
someone to blame
for his past, maybe.
A red letter, at breakfast,
and then shame, a lot of shame. He's got a room that no one enters
where he's drawing circles around words
when he can't sleep and
and then

and now
and who
and how
but no no freeze stop, let me go back!
too many people.
too many options.
gone gone
it's too recent, too accurate
I need to go back.
I erase the crowd
I erase the past
too much to know and handle and knots untied
and I erase the dreams and hobbies and nightmares going wild
and actually let's erase the man and the house
and the wife
and the desk
and what do I have left?
Me. My room. My worlds. Empty bottles and too many dreams.

I go to sleep,
I'm tired,

it's not about him.

There is hope for us

I think there is hope for us,
if we learn to clean the windows better

the kitchen is still a mess
and my bed might fall apart any second now

but don't worry, love,
I'll leave and sell whatever is needed

and if you need storage for future space
I can cut some weight, shrink and reshape

I've done it all before. I know the
rules; I wrote them myself. See,

I take myself apart for people I wish to fit,
and I've got plenty of tactics.

Did you know that if you chew a cube
of ice the hunger pains fade

and did you know
that the dizziness goes away if you run

for a while, and did you know

that people swallow excuses like drugs
and it's a fun game if you play it well
like I do.

Anyway, I'll take care of my monsters

if you take care of the basement

and I think there is hope for us
if we can learn to fit
each other
better
like
hey
make a wish, like 1–2–3
a character I'll learn to be.

_____

constant urge to run away
to start over
to erase everything i've ever done and been
or been with.

Did I write myself lonely?

I can exchange my sadness with words. Like this: some sort of field (a rice field?), a white sky, a colorful bird flying above you when you look up, stretched wings, like he's just floating there. you're somewhere tropical and a kind woman brings you a coffee. you smile and she puts her hands together, her way of honoring you. you like that, you feel welcomed even though you're far from home. there's a fountain in the middle of the scenery and the sound of it is becoming a meditative mantra as you sit there and get things done, on your own. you're productive in your own world and you don't think about someone leaving you.

Did you see it? In front of your eyes?

I did not feel sadness when I wrote that. I felt calm and excited and I can't wait to sit there and write at some point in my life. And now I'm excited to survive until I get there.

Can I write myself out of love? With someone who does not love me back? I surely can write myself into love—I do it all the time. I write myself in love with places and moments, characters and someone's issues. It's lovely.

How long until the sadness comes back once I've stopped writing?
Right away. It comes back right away. Unless I write something magnificent and profound that feels bigger than the sadness
or the love
which is the goal, I guess.
To write something that takes up more space than the sadness.

How to be alone

1. Sit in a room with people who look like you and dress like you, talk like you and sound like you, but still have nothing to say. Watch how they make laughs come as easy as a new day and slowly feel yourself get more invisible with each breath.
Learn what it feels like to not belong.

2. Accept you're a misfit and decide that from now on you don't need those friends, you're just going to make it through your own day without bothering anyone. Wear slick and simple clothes, no colors, no lipstick. Don't tell your stories or ask unnecessary questions. Do what you came to do and go home.

3. Build up your own world, a little outside of the real one, behind closed doors where no one can come in. Collect things you love in there, that no one else has to love. Find music and books, paintings and art. Find a new voice that sounds soothing on its own, learn to whisper, to make a conversation, but not loud enough for anyone to hear. Learn to not feel lonely, just alone.

4. Completely give up the real world and move into your new one. Stop returning calls, stop showing up. Learn to walk with elegance and softness out on the streets. Grow the feeling of a comforting blanket around you, knowing you're not a part of this world anymore, and it can't harm you.

5. Move into your madness, your insanity, your anxious state of solitude and curse it but love it, hate it but need it. You no longer know how to take a place in this world.

6. One day, soft and quiet, find someone who sits lonely on the park bench too, feeding bread to the birds. Smile at him, say hi, ask to sit next to him.

7. Take his hand and go home.

The only way to be alone is to be so together.

Lessons in Love Nr. 2

This lesson is about loneliness.

This is nothing new in my books—I've written four books about standing by the ocean feeling lonely—but it's important to bring this up now, now that I am not lonely anymore, now that I can see the cause and effect and how to get out.

I was not lonely when I met my person. I was alone, but not lonely. I was independent and unstoppable. I was everywhere and nowhere, had people I called my friends, but something changed during those years with my person and I'd like to dissect that because I think it's important. Also, my person is obviously not my person anymore but let's call him something pretty so we all can fall in love with him for at least a little while, like I did, and then you can let him go.

Let's take a trip into our brains, okay?
Every morning as you wake up, there is this tiny instant when your mind is not yet fully aware of where you are or who you are or what you were thinking about before you fell asleep last night. So you, without thinking, quickly run through your past as if to remind your subconscious where you are. "I went through this, I experienced that, this happened to me, that did not happen to me. I'm sad about this, I'm sad about that." Great, now you remember who you are. Because YOU are only whatever story you tell yourself. You meet a new person and all she sees is this pure, wonderful person and she says "hi" and then you open your mouth and your voice will either be confident or nervous, depending on what your brain tells you you are that second, and this new person will slowly get an impression of you that is created by you.

So I moved to a city where I did not know anyone, and I wanted one person to be my world, but he was busy with his own. I felt rejected and forgotten and as I woke up each morning I no longer told myself, "I'm independent and unstoppable," which I still was, by the way, I just got more quiet about that part of myself and my person didn't think I was. He told me I was pretty negative and complained a lot, his voice growing stronger while mine got very weak. He told me this over and over until one morning I simply woke up and said, "I think I'm pretty small and I complain a lot and I'm not so very fond of my life and I don't think my person loves me a lot and I don't think anyone else loves me a lot either." How could I possibly meet another person with this story around me and expect them to leave that conversation feeling inspired and like they belong, like we all want to feel after a conversation with someone?

Okay, so our heroine has changed her story about herself, and stepped into the story that her person tells her about herself. She began to repeat that story to herself, as a reminder of who she was, and slowly that's who she became.

This is all psychology. Have you ever heard about those experiments where a group of people was asked a simple question, like, "What is 1+1?". The first person proudly answers "2", but then the next person answers "7". Our first person laughs a bit, thinking that's a stupid answer. But then one by one they all answer 7 and guess what happens? The first person gets so unsure about his own intellect and abilities and uses his logical reasoning to believe that if all the other people agree that 1 plus 1 equals 7, that must be right. So he changes his answer, questioning everything he's ever known.

This is how we work. You believe something until someone else tells you something different in a really convincing way, time after time, and sooner or later you will simply start to believe it yourself.

So our heroine tried to make a home in another person who also made her believe that she was small and flawed, and she sometimes confided in him saying she felt really lonely but then immediately regretted saying it because that was also a complaint?

Vastness

Quiet Monday, watching the people make their way to buses and trains, cars and schools. It rained last night, washing the streets clean. I wake up early, always, put on the coffee, open the windows, making friends with my heart. How are we today? Gentleness.
I'll go out for a walk later, while the air is still clean and pure, while the birds sing, while it feels like I can still grow so much, become whoever I want. Nothing I can't do! I need to capture this feeling early 'cause it fades through the day.

At night I sit in my kitchen watching the people come back home. Walking with friends, a coffee after work, a lover, a hand to hold. They look happy or stressed, sometimes both. I sip my coffee and live in all this space around me. So much space. I can move and breathe and leave and start anew and it's a privilege I've fought for, cursing it every night now.

This space. What to do with all this space.

How to be a writer

"How do you become a writer?"

20 messages every day...
Simple ... you write?
How do you become a poet?
You write poems...
?
Does having a book deal turn you into more of a "real" writer??

no

it gives you a marketing budget to promote your writing
which is great
if you want to have more time writing
but you're a writer as long as you write
and let me tell you, the "writers" on the billboards
spend more time doing photo shoots and interviews
than writing.

Anyway.
I'm not on any billboards,
I'll answer your messages one by one; I have nothing else to do,
but write,
I guess,
but the answer is still:
"write".

Someone once told me that art becomes art the moment you share a
creation with another soul, and they embrace it and turn it into art.
"Art" that stays in your bedroom is just a hobby. Just a creation.
Art needs a receiver.

I like that idea.
Hobbies are great, but art is fucking beautiful.

Create something and share it with people.
It doesn't matter what happens after that. Just share it and move on. Create something new. There is at least one soul out there, maybe in Mexico, or Sweden, or Singapore, who will stumble upon it one day and relate and seek you out, and that's the purpose of art. To put stuff out there in the universe that didn't exist before.

I don't know... I'm not so educated about these things but ... everyone's talking about politics and world issues but then there's a white, racist, sexist rich man who's ruling the largest empire and I'm just thinking ... they take and take but artists ... we put out? We create and just let it be. We don't ruin. We don't tear apart. We don't take; we give.
We don't exclude.
We simply create and put out and let anyone who needs to find it find it and we'll be happy living simple if we can keep creating.
I think that's beautiful.

In times like these
I think art is noble.
I think art is beautiful.

Journal IV

… me in this place and the distance to you, to him, to her, to them. Am I too far away? Should I come closer? A little to the right? Am I taking up too much space? Should I take up more? What about the color of this T-shirt, is it right? Does it blend in, or stand out, and what would you prefer? Hey, I got a letter from someone the other day and it was beautiful and said sweet words about my art and music and he told me about another continent where he lives and maybe we could go there some time and … oh no more time, sure thing, I'll move a little to the right a little to the back, yes yes I'll leave the key when I go…

I mess up the years that have passed because I should be so much better than this. I was proud of my tender years and now they slip away each day here. I cut my hair and read my books and the people close to me go off on their own and my path is still out there, waiting for someone to occupy it, use it up. Maybe tomorrow. Maybe tomorrow.

I make the bed each day here.
I think I still have time to be.

Constant state of moving on

It takes so much longer to learn to live with yourself than it takes to learn to live with another person. You adapt quickly to each other. Compromise your preferences. Staying up longer, sleeping in, even though you love mornings. You turn vegan, you use less make-up, keep your hair down, like he likes, he says.

It's all good. It's all fine.

Until you learn to keep quiet. Say, "I'm sorry" without knowing what for, hear yourself saying, "I can change, I'll learn." Then you do change. Rearrange everything you ever knew and were and then he leaves. Wasn't enough. "Too late." "Need time alone."

And there you are again. Stranded in an empty room, an "apartment" they tell you, but it looks more like jail. An empty room where you're supposed to spend your life now. "Your home". You live here. This is all you own.

This is your life. This is how you spend your days. There are your people. You sit in a corner hugging your knees tight to your chest wishing someone could find you and take your hand, lead you home, say, "Everything's gonna be fine."

It takes so much longer to learn to live with yourself than it takes to learn to live with another person. You adapt quickly to each other. But how do you adapt to yourself?

Maybe you don't? Maybe you don't *adapt* to yourself? Maybe you *create* yourself. You shape yourself like an architect. Building from the inside out. Characteristics. Interests. Looks. Style.

You build yourself and you don't compromise. You don't change your habits. You want to be someone who wakes early? Start getting up early. Don't think twice about it.

You want to be someone who works out?

You start going to the gym. Don't think twice about it.

You don't have to be happy all the time. You don't have to enjoy every single season of your life. Sometimes you just have to get through and survive, building yourself up in the process. Growth doesn't always equal happiness, but it will in the long run.

Sometimes you just need to turn that heart off and get to work.

Modern love

i'm not trying to be cute, i'm trying to be honest.

I said that to a boy I was writing a song with the other day but he
seemed to prefer something cute than honest
blah blah
I just find it tiring. Pretty things everywhere singing cute things, like,
I'd rather tell you a truth that is ugly and dirty
than a lie that would make me cute.

I don't think I'm really happy yet and sometimes I think money will
make me happy but does no money really make me unhappy?
Sometimes I want to become something that no one thinks is cool
so I could become really great at it and be the best at something and I
wouldn't really care that no one thinks it's cool because I would know
that I was great at it.

I don't need people to see me anymore. I can play you my music, but
I don't need you to like it. I don't need you to read my words or
watch my speeches. I just want to do it. whatever. I can be something
else but I'm gonna keep writing anyway.

Can you become really really great at something if you don't need
anyone else to think you're really really great?
Like, I want to be a really really great writer, but I don't need you to
agree with me.
Do you think Bukowski cared? Do you think Anaïs Nin would have
stopped writing her diary if someone had told her she wasn't a good
writer? or Petrarch, do you think he would have stopped writing his
366 sonnets, to write himself out of heartbreak, if someone had told
him he had no future career as a writer?

No, he wrote 'cause he needed to and that's the only reason he's studied and researched in every literature course on the planet 646 years after his death.

Yeah, I do this. Learn meaningless details about great writers because I find them great and think maybe one day i can be one of them. Write something really really great and be studied by people who prefer something honest than pretty.

I don't think very many pretty things make me feel a lot but the truth always does. I also don't think i'm really very happy yet but writing always makes things better. It won't make me any money but does no money really make me unhappy if I at least can write every day?

I think I'll be happier writing with no money than not writing with a lot of money.

Dark love

He's pretty when he smiles and I'm learning not to drink straight from the bottle. Words get to me deeper when I'm sober and I wish I could wear a cape of pretty colors that make the words bounce back, like a shield of protection; some kind of glass. A broken piece of glass, so the light still gets through, but not the words, the opinions, the ugly thoughts.

I have a headache but tell myself I'm just lazy. I can't sleep and tell myself I should stop drinking. I'm worried and scared about the future, about money, about the next rent
and yell to myself to just grow the fuck up.

Hey, I'm talented and I CAN achieve things. If I just make the decision. So shut up and let me do this thing my way 'cause I don't need your help and you don't understand this anyway!

Hey, I'm sorry, please come back, I'm scared and alone and I need you and … I don't know how to speak. Can I write you a poem? A song? I am still sorry.

Sometimes I wonder how anyone could ever understand what I'm trying to say here. But I think sometimes someone does, and sometimes even more than me because I get thoughtful responses to my words and songs, developed longer and deeper, and that makes it all worth it.

Sometimes you're so quiet, are you still out there? Does this help you? Am I making something worthwhile? Nothing makes me happier than feeling like I'm helping. I could use some help myself but most of all I want to help you so if you can't afford my book, my music, a place to stay, come here, here, I'm here. My couch is a bit small but enough to rest on and I will listen and understand and you can borrow my hoodie if you get cold? You're not alone. Am I?

I just want to know you. Are you there?

The Doorway

I stood in your doorway this morning
dreaming you'd turn around.
you'd tilt your head.
you'd whisper softly "stay"

or that you'd grab my arms
to shake me while asking
what the hell are we doing
we love
each other
and this is not right
so we will make this work
now stay!

You poured your coffee. Stirred the spoon like a crystal man
with your back to me and not a sound. the fridge humming elegies
while the clock ticked on
and the streets are so clean here people rushing to work
and maybe I should be too
by now
at this age
this stage
this town.

I will stand in that doorway
dreaming
for many nights to come.

Loneliness is only lonely if you let it be

November comes again and the man across the street shovels leaves like meditation. I expect to be lonely when the dark falls, but I also expect a hand to hold and neither seems just right this year. I turn my day around to escape the nights. I wake up at 4 a.m. because the sadness doesn't come until later and I want to be asleep before it does.

I could just leave. I could just call it finished, say the season is over, thank you for the memories, get up and leave. It would be simple. I would love it. The feeling as I walk home today would be so different. Liberated. Like a burden falling off my shoulders because somehow I did not know, but learned, that the sacrifices and good deeds you try to do for another person can turn into heavy weights for them, too. Too heavy to carry. And the "thank you" I hoped to find each morning, from someone I thought I helped out, was replaced by "why" and questions, silence even. Telling me to stop.

I did just try to love him. I did just try to act with serenity and heart. I did just try to see how I was free as a bird and he was not so I could fly to him and pictured it wonderful. He would greet me with open arms and say, "Thank you for coming back!" and he would take me in and show me his house. Say, "You can sleep here and this is your chair, where we'll have coffee in the morning and long sober talks at night, and I will show you around." I would smile and feel loved and love in return because I would feel appreciated for the sacrifice I made … for us?

Instead, he asked me why, said it's heavy when I'm here. I found myself hurrying home every morning by myself full of shame and regrets, sadness and anger,

because how stupid could I be to think someone could love
in the way I love
and how stupid could I be to think I had the right

to count on someone,
rely on someone,
and how stupid could I be to think someone
would want to build a nest
with me.
a home
with me.
the most homeless of them all who never seems to learn.
I'm no one to build homes with, only temporary moments of
whatever I can offer in the moment and I forgot that and tried to be
settled. available. but people don't want that. They want fragmented
moments of me, only at my best, preferably twice a year when they're
bored of ordinary.

Anyway. I'm fine. It's November and I'm writing lists of things to see
now. I'd like to go to Prague again. I'd like to go to Paris. Berlin is
nice in the fall. I just bought a piano ... I'll sell it on eBay.
Loneliness is only lonely if you let it be.

Journal V

At first it was northern lights and soft songs in the morning.
Now it is ignoring the dishes until they pile up and watching *Mad Men* because I'm too old to get fucked up and we need some escape.
I paid my dues but they keep following me, like a son I never had but he keeps telling me I'm his mother and I keep saying "I'M NOT YOUR MOTHER, LEAVE ME ALONE" but who really cares. You're always the person someone decides you to be.

No one listens anymore. I introduced myself with 5 different names tonight and no one gave me a second glance. I could be whoever I want to be, I think. We could all be stars, no one would doubt it. Blindly swallowing the need for celebrity glitter and famous living but I just want it simple. I just want it all back. Northern lights and soft songs in the morning. No more *Mad Men* or dishes piling up because we're too busy, too lazy, too fucked up to
get going.
I just want it simple.
I just simply want it all.

Masks

It's your bones against mine.
The slight curve in your spine
and it's Sunday:
I don't have to think about suicide.

I see the world in black and white,
but there's shift
around you
and the music is intense but distant,
a vague memory of a song I once knew.

I adjust the way I say I live
to suit your mode
and I adjust the way I speak my mind
to suit your mode
and Sweden is my home, love, yes yes
I am safe and calm now
no more worries, pour that liquor down my throat.

No, no, let me take that back—
you're weak and cold, your cowardly way of taking a year to right a
wrong
and fuck you for still contributing to elegies
when you've already written the ending
and fuck you for being so horribly
sweet
that I just
can't
leave.

Love affair

I am replacing 'romance' with 'love affair' in the poems about us for
we were never a romance
but a deal, tied and sealed, not to be adjusted.
You kept your hands firm over my mouth
as not to touch
or speak
just show
and I knew I could never ask for more.

(I would never ask for more.)

I was a hiding place at best.
Repeating sighs like "thank you"
after every 'affair' of making 'love'
and I was a playground,
providing jokes and faults and other thoughts
and maybe you enjoyed it for a while
and so did I
but I will always be your hiding place
at best.

This is our affair collapsing under our feet.
Two cities on common ground
but I'm dreaming of landslides and we're slipping further away.
Let me rephrase that:
I am standing sure on the shore, waving my hands and telling you
that
I
am
not
leaving.

He loved me some days. I'm sure he did.

But this was never my country,
somehow only yours to keep
so you split the land
and now you push me out to sea,
me thinking I'm standing strong and sure
at the shore.

You're making me leave
so you can stay.

You are telling me to leave
and still will tell of how I left.

Madness

I'm daydreaming. I'm talking to people who do not exist and I'm going mad in my own madhouse. Can isolation open doors, or does it just close them? Do you open the door to an extended world of madness and hallucinations, or does the door back to reality close on you and you're stuck in your own mind?

They say if you spend too much time in solitude you can enter a state of calm anxiety. The line between what's being said in your mind and outside of it fades away, all blurs into one and you can no longer distinguish a real sound from an imagined one.

I wrote a song today and recorded it, sang it from the bottom of my lungs and it was beautiful and great and I couldn't wait to tell people that I'm up again. I'm alive! Walking, breathing, eating, singing: I'm back! But then I turn my computer on and my inbox is empty, no activity for 5 days and I stay silent.

I'm daydreaming, talking to people who do not exist and I don't know where the door is.

mad people, mad people everywhere, and I'm one of them.

loneliness is eating me alive. I'm going mad in my own mind.

Lessons in Love Nr. 3

This is the part where sadness turns into anger, because it always does. Right?

See, no one really has the right to cross a certain line. You know that line, where it's no longer about someone saying something to you from the outside; it's about them now reaching for an inner subconscious spiritual invisible soulful layer of your being, commenting on who you are as a human, where you're from and your history and your culture and your class. This is a layer no one ever has the right to have opinions about. That's called respect. Manners. Being raised well and the second someone crosses over and reaches for that layer you know they're only out to offend you and you, with your pure conscience and higher standards, will simply walk away.

Can we all just resolve to first of all never reach for that layer in others, and second of all, respect ourselves enough to walk away when someone else does? Yes? Great.

There is enormous power in just walking away, and there are certain situations when that is your right. Now don't stretch it—there are many layers before this where you will have standards and strength and manners enough to stay. To listen, to try to understand, to explain yourself with intellect and calm. But you know the difference, don't you? You've been there. I think we all have.

This is the part where I should have looked my person in the eye and calmly but decisively said, "I am going to leave this now. This is no longer serving me. Goodbye."

So why did I not? Why did he not?

We were two good people stuck in a sad story and no one felt hope or belonging but no one had the strength to walk away. Why?

Maybe because we're beings who want to believe in happy ever after so badly that we just refuse to accept that this is not it. Maybe tomorrow? Maybe we're just tired? Maybe one day? So I go to sleep after another fight, his back against mine, me staring into his wall. I'm angry and offended, feeling rejected and misunderstood, but I still love him. How?

Him, sitting on the couch a month later, not looking at me, not talking, strumming a guitar, being a different person.

I fell into a conversation a while ago with a new friend, who sees me not as someone negative but as someone nice, I think. Anyway, he said that maybe it's a male way of handling chaos: you turn off completely. You go on autopilot, trying not to feel or think anything at all. While the yin way to handle tragedy is to desperately reach for salvations and ways to make things right or better or new or okay. We refuse to accept anything, ever, and we want so desperately to hold on to things that we even hold on to broken relationships and closed chapters.

I don't put gender on feelings but I do acknowledge the Earth and the Sky. Water and fire. Yin and yang. And I know we have a lot to learn from both. Anyway, let's move on.

I've been gone for so long

1. I have learned to repeat people's names when they introduce themselves like:
"I'm Eric."
"Hi, Eric."
And I've learned to show an intriguing but safe smile to make them feel like they know me enough to not ask my name again.

2. I'm introducing myself with different names because no one asks twice or mentions it again.

3. I used to be interested in human interactions. Relationships of all sorts intrigued me because I always found myself on the outside. Someone forgot to give me the key, or the code, and I watched them discover each other, like maps written on skin and I observed like a researcher. Who sat next to whom, who stood a little too close by the bus stop. It taught me silence. I didn't want to be involved, just understand.

4. The lonely sound of keys from a computer at a library. It makes my heart break.

5. It's June and the mornings are quiet. Still, I put the headphones on and write until there's nothing left to say.
I think there's a concert here tonight. I wish they wanted me to play and not just listen.
I still sing on stages every night in my head.

6. I think I could make someone's day. I think I could be pretty exciting again, for someone.
I think I could start fires and explosions in someone's chest and bring them to libraries and small unknown paths in the forest. I would

reveal myself slowly, outer to inner, with no rush. Keep it sacred. I would fall asleep holding them just tight enough to let them know they matter. Like a whisper saying, "I'd like to be here for you."

I think I could be exciting again.

7. Does anyone miss me? I've been gone for so long.

I want a second chance

This urge for aloneness—this chamber around my heart that I just can't escape—what did it ever do for me? Well, see, sir, I'm an artist of creations, and the process of creating demands stability, in and around. A quiet world, to hear my thoughts, and I built my process in a still state of mind, far off from others.

I walk through the town, where I live, and the people feel distant and not quite full-blooded enough because they don't get to me.

Nothing really gets to me.

I want a second chance. I'd do things better, be more precise. I'd build it all up from the ground again with better material and stronger hands. I'd choose a better spot, in the sun, in the spring, and I would smile from fulfillment, never mistaking the right choice for a pleasant one.

I want a second chance: I should have gone right instead of left and this time I'll make it right. I'd be better. More defined. Clearer. Sharper edges. Always precise.

I want more for my art. I want more for my audience. I long for greater magic and longer intervals of pure artistic freedom and I want more for everyone involved. No commercial success: a DEEPER success. I want to mean so much more to everyone.

I want to mean so much more to someone.

I'd like to be a bit more for myself. Feel a bit more. Expand a bit more.

The only way out is through.

I still have time to be.

I am still here. That is enough.

it feels like …

people around me tell of achievements and glory. they grew up and climbed their ladders,

collected friends and belongings, leveled up and signed contracts

while i sat on the other side of the table thinking … i failed. i did not make it. i've been angry and frustrated, saw no way out and no way in, and i was simply left on the outside.

but this morning i walked by the water and i sat down and watched the sun rise over the mountains, and i remember sitting there at 14 years old wanting to never see it again. wanting

to enter that water, step by step and

i did not want to be in this body anymore. i did not want to take on the challenge of creating myself,

or accepting myself, facing the simple terror of all things worldly.

but i went on and kept going, even when i thought i couldn't

and maybe i never got the contracts and the glory

but i got the privilege of learning how many ways a mind can trick you and cheat you and slowly slowly, little by little, befriend you. not throw so many dark thoughts or ugly words about all there is to think about oneself

and it threw me on journeys i never knew existed.

it showed me music and landscapes, books and philosophy.

it taught me healing and human behavior

and my biggest achievement is that i am still here. doing what i do.

learning every single day how to be a good person

and i still act out of anger sometimes,

but i have hope in myself to be good for someone one day.

i live and i create and i find small things every day to fall in love with

and i might not have much but i feel so full most of the time

and i am still here.

i too want it all. i too want the dreams and the goals and the smiles at
the finish line. but most of all
i just simply want to be
here.
i am proud of being tired and unsure but going out into the world
anyway. facing the crowd, the mic, the blank page ... anyway.
and i am proud for pretending like nothing else.

Journal VI

You're the one I want to share all this with. The pleasures and the pains and I wonder if you can sleep at night, and if not; how come? What do you think about? Are you happier than ever before? And do I have anything to do with it? Or am I just one in the line; you could find something, or someone, else to fill my absence if I pack up and leave? I want to tell it all, to you, but still, I have nothing to say.

The silence spreads and we go through our shallow ways, as if to describe the possessions in our bags, and my throat tightens, trying to remember what I used to tell this man, whose voice I hardly recognize, now, after all these years.

Did we both change? a little too differently?
Did you change, and I not? Or the other way around?
Is this all in my head?

Would we be happier finding a way to fit into each other's differences, or would we be happier going our separate ways?

I have nothing to tell you.
Where do I start?

Joke's on me

"Babe," he said, "when are you gonna slow down?"
I did not understand the question and laughed a little, insecure, like always, and pondered on.

My heart is always racing so fast and I think I'm excited. There are so many things I'd like to get to. Places; feelings; people. I have to go I have to go don't have time sorry sorry have to go
and off I go, running for the new thing, the new aim, the new goal.
But when do you get there? Did I ever get anywhere?
I leave so fast I'm not sure. People cleaning up the mess I always leave behind. I close my eyes and ponder on, telling myself I'm off for a new start, another adventure. But how do you really finish something?

There was a lovely pond where I used to live a little bit outside of Bristol. I ran along it every morning but I never stopped and took it in. I remember pieces of my life like fragmented photographs appearing before my eyes. I want to go back to it all, to all those places I walked but never fully walked because I was always on my way somewhere. Running away away away and off I go
and now then, where do you wanna go now? You won't be there anyway, you know. Where are you going? You'll never get there.

I drink too much and I cancel plans one after the other. I want more people in my life but I'm too scared to lose them so I make no attempt. I do not reach out.
My throat is sore. I run, I sing, I clean my apartment.

joke's on me. i'll take it if you give me one.

Go lightly

I wake up some mornings just feeling ... frail. Like, please be careful, go slow, don't touch me too roughly, speak gently.

It happens after worried nights, reliving things from the past or dreaming things I don't wish to happen, and I wake up feeling unrested and sore. Like I've been pushed around between two thorny edges and my mind is as wounded as my body and the sky is as fragile as me, about to break into tears any moment.

I used to run out in a worried state of anxiety, not knowing where to go with my body on these days, not knowing how to drown out the strange unrest in my chest and I used to run run run until it felt better, which it rarely did, until the day was done and I could leave it behind and move on.

PROOF But I'm learning to be gentle with myself. To treat myself with the same care I wish others to. So I don't push, I don't force. I make myself something warm to drink, I sit down in a sunny spot, feeling the warmth like a safety blanket. I read something comforting, something about my place in the universe and how there is a constant line of energy piercing through, a constant source of well-being, and I just have to tune into it, I just have to close my eyes and breathe it in.

I go for a slow walk, I listen to music I like. I call a friend and ask how he is, how his mum is, if work is going well. I go to the cinema by myself and watch something bubbly and happy because it makes me feel better, to not take it all so seriously, and I walk home alone in the dark, slowly once again, because I go gently and if I'm not strong some days I adjust the pace and slow down, for myself.

I think the key is to lose the fixed, unbroken standard of how a human being should feel and look and get on with each and every day like a robot in a factory. You're not a robot. You're a delicate, living, moving, human particle of energy, and your energy comes and goes and it's all okay. Don't push so hard. Listen to your heart and adjust your pace to its beating.

Every day has a different rhythm. If you go faster than what's meant for you today you'll step out of the beat. You'll go out of the flow. Ease into it. Go lightly.

CLOSE ONE DOOR TO OPEN ANOTHER

I will be a writer now

Someone once said, "Get your heart real good and broken and you'll be a poet for the rest of your life." Well, I don't actually know if someone ever said this but I hope someone did 'cause I would like to hear it. I would like to know that this pain will last for good reasons and that my words will come back through it

'cause I've been dry on words like a prayer in the desert, no life or sign of spark. I've lived so nicely, so slowly, making my way towards something I never really knew what, but it was so nice, to slow down. To not flee, just stay. A quiet living. A quiet street. I have lived so nicely.

I expected a catastrophic chaos and all kinds of awful, but my heart is strangely quiet.

There is a quiet peace even in the loudness of a heart breaking. There is a strange sense of acceptance, like nodding my head to myself, saying, *it's alright, it's alright, you're doing fine*. Maybe I'm just older. Been here before, know my way out. Maybe it's quietly dying— sometimes I feel like I am. Either way, how does 'alive' feel? But I know I can't go back, only forward, no use in fighting, so onwards I go, a little every day, and I do the best I can.

It comes in waves, mostly at night. Dreams and memories resurfacing and I wake up cold and tired, lonely in a vast sea of sadness. how can the lack of someone feel so large? how can the lack of someone feel so heavy? it's December and the early evenings are so dark.

My brain jumps in and out, hopeful to devastated. I'm crying but I'm so so happy. I'm sorry, but I'm so grateful. For the lessons. For the growth.

I should have focused on being a writer. I used to write quite well, I think? I had a lot to say, a lot to think about. I think a lot of people could relate. I got letters and gifts back then, people saying "thank you". I should have kept to my words, kept writing to people and for people and maybe I could have been someone for someone. You know, one of those you turn to when you're in pain.

But i'm back again, feeling things, staying up with the moon, listening to the same old songs, like back then, when i wrote, all the time, saying things, reaching out. Maybe I can be someone now, for someone. Maybe I can write myself out of this one too, like I've done so many times.

I will be a writer now. I will say it all.

Erased

It's like that song we both loved and used to listen to, both together and apart, and every time I hear it now I wonder if you think of me when you hear it, too?

Did I leave some kind of scar? A vessel from your past to your now? and about that last night, grasping fingers in the dark—did it feel like an ending, or a fresh start?

I wonder where you are now. memories fading fast.

You loved me some days. I'm sure you did.

You loved me some days, when the sun shone high in the sky.

Your steps were light and easy, dancing naked in the bathroom. I laughed and you laughed and we talked like kids do, unashamed and open for joy, barely bothered by the rain coming. Your eyes were clear and genuine some days. Mostly when other people were around. Sometimes when only I was.

I will remember those days.

You loved me some days.

Said my name in that way I fell in love with, like it mattered and meant something. But I'm not who I was those years ago and you only want to see who I was then, refusing to explore who I've become now.

So we had to learn tenderness, lightly touching the wounds we'd caused each other. Hearts bruise so easily on this side of town and wounds heal so slowly.

You never told me your dreams. I never knew you fulfilled them. I never knew.

I stayed up some nights hoping the phone would ring, that maybe you would share them with me. Your dreams. I never knew you fulfilled them.

There was a thick cloud hanging over Lisbon and we sat by the water, the wind playing with your hair. I kept my eyes on the horizon, like I always do, holding back a thick stone in my throat, like I always do. Sometimes your voice gets so distant. I zoom out and fly somewhere far away. Somewhere brighter and lighter where I'm something stronger than this broken character you keep turning me into and I just want to move on. Somewhere far away. Somewhere someone can look at me like maybe I'm doing okay. Like maybe I'm pretty good?

Maybe somewhere, someone can look at me with new eyes and let me start over and see what I've become, now, after all those years, unaware of how I was back then.

Can wounds really heal? Will someone give me a second chance? Maybe I am better now? Maybe I am strong and happy and light and simple. No more stones in my throat or escape routes at night.

I thought we made it through. The storm left us stronger than ever before. But he told me we didn't. Said it's all too broken, too many things we said that we can't unsay and I kept my eyes on the horizon holding back the stone in my throat like I always do and I tried keeping bright things on my mind. Brighter days like I know are coming. "I'll be fine, I'll be fine," knowing I will, in a while at least.

I'm too lonely, he says. Too goddamn lonely. Too broken to be fixed and now I wander yet another Christmas in a foreign country wondering how things went so wrong. Am I really that bad? How did I get so goddamn lonely that even love can't heal it and where do you go to start over and get a new chance? I just want someone who looks at me without seeing something sad. I just want someone who looks at me like maybe I'm okay. Like maybe I'm pretty good?

You loved me some days, when the sun shone high in the sky. I'll remember those days. I'll keep them close and dear.

You loved me some days.

You're still doing just fine

It's midnight. I turned the music off to not wake the neighbors up. Every fifth minute a lonely car passes by. I made a list to push you on, you need it:

1. I know the last year was unkind, weighing you down though you tried hard to stay flying. Stubborn like a dreamer in the sky. It's over now, kid. Things will get better.
You made it through.

2. What do you learn from loving someone?
You learn to let go when it's time.
Did you let go yet? Did you love him a little more?
Keep loving, keep letting go. Don't stop.

3. You keep searching for something to do, something you're good at. Something that makes people stop and say, "You're good at this!"
and this is it.
Words. That's it. Stick to your words, kid. They flow as easily as a breath and they have since your very first one and they always come back, saving you when you no longer know where to go or what to do and you can arrange them as easily as 1–2–3
and you don't even have to think, you see?
Stick to those words, kid. Write it all down, what happens after is not your business now. Just write it all. The stories; the novels; the poems; the thorns.
Finish *Persuasion*, I think it will do you good.

4. The music is always there. You sing but no one can hear. Stop searching for an audience so desperately. The audience will come when you learn to let go. Close your eyes and sing, that's all you can do.

5. Where do you go when you can go everywhere? Where do you start?

The answer is little by little. One step forward and go from there. You'll find it soon, kid. Just go where you can, today, and you'll get somewhere one day.

6. It's not what you thought and it's not what you hoped for, but it's all good. It's all okay.

This silence now

I look out the window and wish for
something——anything,
but this silence
now.

I miss you, dear.
I miss you always in the morning
brushing my teeth
and I miss you always in the evening
preparing my meal
and I miss you always at night
unable to sleep.
I miss you all the fucking time

and my mind is an orchid.
I'm painting it beautifully
with all kinds of art
and there are fairies and dancers
and painters
and laughter,
but go a bit further.
Find the right corner of my mind
and you will find a spot there
that no one occupies.
I kept it reserved
and painted it in all kinds of art
and I kept it for you.
That place
is for you.

I woke up to the flutes

from the church
down my street
and I walked around the building for two hours
unable to go inside
for my body is gritty and full of sin and no one should witness
me
now
like this.

I look out the window and wish for
something—anything,
but this silence
now.

Unpoetic

Some days, there is no poetry. The rain is not pretty and the sun is too bright. The lake is still and I close my eyes and wish for something to change inside me. But some days there is no change in sight. Only a painful tugging at the heart, refusing to go away, making it hard to eat or sleep, write or read and I want to flip my life around, a 360 switch and start a new chapter. There is no life around here. All life is gone.

Someone left me and I have no one around. I walk lonely, trying to keep bright things in mind. Like my art. Like my passions. My plans and dreams and all the oceans left to sail,
but today there is no poetry. The stillness is not pretty.

People come and go all the time but I've built a castle around me, making it hard for anyone to enter. I just want to feel safe. I just want to be fine.
But then someone leaves and I am alone and now I wish for nothing more than people people all kinds of people to come into my castle where we can sit in a ring and hold hands and tell stories and keep warm. Everyone would be welcome. Everyone would just love each other and I would heal. slowly. remembering all the things I've written before. but it's so hard now. poetry says so little some days. but i know it will, soon, again.

I have no one around so I talk to myself, turned the mic on one night and somewhere on the way I formulated proper thoughts and real ideas, and my heart felt a little better after every hour and I fell in love with the thought that maybe by sharing the things that keep me up at night, I could help someone else, maybe? Or just, have a conversation with you? If you care? I would love to let you in—into my castle—the door is open.

It's like ... I'm sitting on a chair with my hands resting on my legs, palms turned open to the sky. I have so little in me, but I would give you whatever I can. just ... stay? a little? hold my hand? tell me something. Loneliness is so hard when you're left in it.

The Space of Absence

I had never felt it before:
The physicality of how much inward pain can slip and leak through
the cracks of the skin,
the skin I've worked so hard to keep intact, and I'd never felt it before:
the way it was impossible beyond belief to keep sitting
there
in that chair with the people and words and normal conversations
and I did not know where to go with myself.
They were having a lovely evening with dear friends
and isn't it ironic how they see me as one of them
but still know nothing
for I wanted to scream or cry or laugh or run for a thousand miles
with the wolves and the haunted,
or to be haunted,
just a solution to where to put my body with this mind and the
thoughts of him
for everything became related
to him
like company became the absence
of his
and laughter became the lack
of his
and I'd never felt it before.
How loneliness becomes more than just a feeling
and slowly locks itself around your throat and you can physically feel
it.
how it's tightening and thickening
and I had to count to three to not hyperventilate
inhale, exhale, look straight forward, do not scream
don't make a sound.

The others kept talking and eating and drinking
and someone next to me talked about travels
and Sarah made a joke
and Dave smoked his cigarettes
and I was drowning and screaming
but said nothing.
And it scares me still,
how I could sit there and sink like a wreck in the storm
fighting for my life
with no one even flinching,
and I'd never felt it before
the way something snapped inside and flicked my core
and I could not even stand up and walk out
or away
only sit there
counting to three on each breath
until the night was over and the hour late
and I used my last reachable strength to get out of the house and out
on the street
and I kept walking until I was out of sight,
out of mind,
until I fell over in the snow on the ground
the tears in my breath
and the winter all around
but still I felt nothing
except for the hurt
and the absence.

They say there's a pain so profound that it blocks out everything else
and I know it's true because it did
and I had never felt it before
the way you still can kill me
even though it's been months

and it's bigger now,
the mere bones of my body,
for sometimes it has nothing to do with you
or them
only me
and you're just the root
where it all started
and kept spreading
growing like cancer and now it's all over.
Now now it's too late.

I had never felt it before:
How absence can be bigger than presence.
How the lack of something can be heavier than what's there.
How you are a bigger part of me now
than you were when you were here.

He loved me some days. I'm sure he did.

Hospital

I once lay in a hospital myself
praying to keep myself alive
and I've lain on several grounds too
and I know for a fact
it's not very different

praying to get to stay alive
and praying to want to
stay alive.

Lead me to the broken ones

Lead me to the ones who have loved
and lost
and forgotten.
Take me to the ones
who can teach me
how to forget someone you once loved.
Someone you still love.
Because I know what to do, but I don't know how
or why
or when
and I know that I am now one of them
and no longer alone
flailing my arms, standing on on this wreck, sinking.
But you stood cold like a lighthouse,
observing how I slowly drifted out to sea.
Left me wondering if that's the man I love, or loved
or knew.

So now
lead me to the ones who have loved
and lost
and forgotten.
Who can teach me
how to forget

and learn to love again.

I loved you like I always will

I will miss
my chest exploding
you coming home late
not turning on the light
always waking me up

I will miss
the sudden burst of safety
when you look at me
or hold my hand
or say something like
"let's go home"

I will miss
the years I lost
on something or someone
the pieces didn't fit, shaped wrong
the timing slightly off

I loved you like I always will.

Lisbon, 2018

I keep putting myself in solitary places, for the pleasure of it, I think. A brown-eyed boy said hi in Swedish, so I looked down and walked away.

The heat is so constant. It's like a wall as I open the window each morning and it consumes my senses; there is not space enough for sadness or cold. I bought a black dress with a bare back, I wander in sandals and wear no make-up. I let my hair blow free and I only sing before 6 a.m. on wild streets or in front of the ocean, where no one can hear.

They drink sangria at 2 p.m. here, smoke cigars and go to the beach. I walk with a notebook and a collection of poetry under my arm, ignoring texts and emails, pretending I might stay. Pretending I'm not on the run, pretending I live somewhere. My mum asked me how long I'm staying and I replied, "i miss you too".

I could stay here. I could find myself a job, make some friends, find a home near the beach where I would walk every morning. Meditate, slow down and serenade the drinkers at night by the pub.

I have two months of rent in my bank account. My new book sold okay. I paid €100 to bring my guitar overseas and I'm thinking of teaching yoga classes in the parks, if people want to come; donation based.

My life is donation based. Give me what you think I'm worth. How much do you want me to survive? That's not what I mean and not what I say but that's how it feels, some days.

I am in love with the constant struggle. The constant pushing, trying to get by. I am in love with the feeling of making it another month, of simply getting by. I fell into a discussion with a British economics student, told him he spoke from an angle of white privilege and he did not understand the other side of money. He wouldn't live anywhere other than London unless he had a job there so he voted to leave the EU, proud to not be a part of it. I said he was young and not very traveled and I regretted it the second I said it.

My brother is graduating soon. A fine master's in something important. He'll get a nice salary, has a girlfriend, and lives in a nice flat. My ex-boyfriend just got engaged and my old best friend is pregnant.

I'm writing poetry in a beach bar in Lisbon, sipping gin and only need two more songs to fill a new record. I fall asleep to the sound of drunk university students in the room next door, here to party. "Are you a student?" "No, no, I'm here to work," I say. Softly. Smiling. "I think I'm a little older than you."

I met a Norwegian boy who practiced yoga and said he saw rainbows in my eyes. Now he sends me photos from Canada, where he's moving, and I save them on my hard drive to keep as a daydream. As an escape plan. No matter what happens, I still haven't been to Canada. I can still go to Canada.

The heat is so constant. There is no space for anything else.
I can make it another month. Maybe even more.
I don't think I ever asked for more than this.

Lessons in Love Nr. 4

We put aside money for the gym membership and prioritize an hour a day there, because nothing is more important than our physical bodies, right? Mental health is slowly getting the rank it deserves and meditation is not taboo anymore. But tell me one time something has been off in your relationship and it hasn't affected your entire day and life? Tell me you haven't felt how a slight shift in your lover's voice, on the phone, didn't affect your physical body and your mental health and it didn't matter how many hours you spent at the gym or how many breaths you could take with eyes closed while focusing on your nostrils—the shift in voice, in mood, on the phone, took over everything.

Still, we do not prioritize studying psychology, emotional intelligence and how to develop a calm, nourishing, healthy relationship with other people that neither harms nor tires your person or yourself.
How many books have you read on personal development? How many books have you read on peaceful communication in a relationship?

Rilke wrote in *Rilke on Love*: "When you give someone flowers, you arrange them beforehand, don't you? But young people who love each other fling themselves to each other in the impatience and haste of their passion."

Did I arrange myself enough to be a gift for someone? To brighten someone's days, rather than throwing myself in like the storm that I am?
Is this person I'm thinking about inviting into my life arranged enough? Did he put in the work to know what he wants and where he wants to go? Because you can't figure those things out when you're already in it, you need to do this now, alone.

If you see this

I know you're reading this, late, on your phone.

window wide open, one last cigarette before you fall asleep on that couch,

like always, too tired to undo the bed, to finish the day, to make any plans

for tomorrow or the next day,

like always.

I wanted plans. Grand plans! Large plans! Long plans!

I wanted visions and goals, dreams and nostalgia

but you're too tired. You want now, nothing more. You want an open window and another cigarette, smoking it while reading my poems, night after night, to make sure I'm still alive, I'm still okay.

I write to keep my life going, to show I'm still here, feeling things, expanding or shrinking but at least doing something and it's the only way for the people who once were in my life to keep in touch with me in some way. I don't call. I don't answer. I leave or they leave and we move on and now I write.

Landslide

I'm tearing up continents to find
a body that is not full of anger,
a voice that is not strained
or firm,
hands that want well,
no preconceived opinions
about my intentions
when I dare to say things.
I long for a mind that does not shake,
that does not depart when things around me change.
That does not get disappointed
but instead tilts his head and asks:
"Can you explain what you mean?"

I just wanted connection when I felt stranded without anything to
hold on to
but my words were taken and rearranged into a different language
and I was heard as selfish. disrespectful. pessimistic.
I was labeled unexciting when I just wasn't given the chance to show
myself.

I want to find someone who looks at me with good intentions
who would like to like me
who speaks with a warm tone trying to understand.

I want nothing but love, now.

Journal VII

Sweden. 9th of October. The neighbors have escaped for the weekend. Piles of colored leaves, neatly put together and I walk barefoot everywhere, just for the sake of it. I'm back after 8 years of being gone and they don't make them like us anymore. They have electric lawnmowers now, slowly rolling on day and night
in case the grass grows tall
as it does here because the air is clean, maybe.
He said in the car, "Such a boring road,"
and I crumpled my face, thinking, *HOW CAN THIS BE BORING?!*
This is the most wonderful road I have traveled
since I moved out in the world
and there are animals and fields and seven shades of green!
It was the most beautiful road I had traveled in years!

But I don't think I ever really moved. I never stayed anywhere, always left, on and on
and if you ask me where I've been the last 8 years, I'll shrug my shoulders and say:
"Don't know … a bit of everywhere," because that's about as precise as I can be. So now I sit in the grass in October, breathing in calmer air and I just like it here. People are friendlier, always greeting me with a smile no matter the weather,
and the security guy at the club is on my side, wants to protect me,
and the police are always kind, helping and guiding
and my bank man invites me for coffee to give me tips and advice, because it's part of their job here. People are simply nice to me, no one ignoring my English questions
because they're angry they don't speak the language,
and I don't have a lot of friends left but I think I can get new ones. Because people are open to new ideas. And when I say I'm a traveling songwriter and author they find it cool enough to ask a question but

then that's that, nothing special. Just one of the gang. And I like it. No more questions. Just take me as I come.

I keep the television on with no sound. I like the company. Candles and freshly brewed coffee. The neighbor's house lights up at 8 p.m. every night. It's quiet. It's clean.
I don't know, I just like it here.

Back to work:
I work better here. I don't really work but the work I call my work, I do better here. I read better. I write better. The words arrive more easily because there is no pressure of fitting in, or standing out, or proving to someone I'm good enough, and I just sit by my desk by the window and let them come as they are. I sing better, more freely, louder, because no one complains about me singing. I think they like it, even. It's nothing special, really. Everyone kind of sings, maybe I just do it a little louder, more often, about different things. But no more questions: I like it.
I hear my own heart, beating on, I walk and run and go places, see people and it's all a little more joyful, nothing standing in my way.
So … I'm not sure. I think I simply just like it here.

I'm not trying to fool anyone. I don't think my restless heart can be tamed and maybe I'll call a place my home for a while or two but one day I'll up and leave, again, for that's how I'm wired, and I think I like being wired that way. As long as it takes me nice places. Lovely places. With kind people.
Kind people …
People are everything and I want to ask every person I meet a thousand questions but I'm silenced and pushed to the side by people I've lived around for years, not speaking what I speak and I feel left out. Pushed out from the circle of society and systems and orders and

I'm walking on the little circled line outside the Earth because there is no place for me inside it.

Maybe this is my little opening of the circle, back into life, back into Earth. How stupid I would be to keep walking, not entering.

I'll make this work, no matter what

I'm seeing friends again. Laughing easily without excusing my language or accent, without wondering if it was the right thing to say, and I say "I love you" when we go opposite ways, just so they know. Because I haven't said it in so long and it feels important that they know.

I'm finding new bands and songs and books to love again, and there is this forest where I live where wildflowers grow, and I walk there every morning. My days are still lonely for I've chosen a life that has a strange way of flowing, no days or nights, just endless running on and on, but it's okay. I'm okay.

Anyway, I've made a habit of picking fresh flowers every morning because soon it's autumn again and people will stay inside. It will get dark before it gets bright, and I want to make the best of this year, the little left of it. I close my eyes and breathe in deeply, lucky to have made it through. One more time. one more time.

Things are wrong and right at the same time. They're okay, but not right, and maybe they never will be and maybe that's not the point, maybe the point is the very decision to make things work no matter what.

That's what passion does to you. That's what heat and warmth and an undying love for life
do to you.

I'll make this work, no matter what.
That's what I want my undying love for life
to make of me.
I'll make it work, no matter what.

Full circle

I'm in Germany, back to where I started.
It feels like.
I mean, it started in London but brought me to Scotland, Hamburg,
Lisbon, Prague, Barcelona, but I'm here again,
closing another round. Another story for the book and I'm drinking
whisky
by myself
again
trying to be a writer.

If I had a publisher I would have a team, people who counted on me.
Asking me for the script, the progress, the profit. I would have to
show the work put in, write for numbers, tell the stories. "Write
longer, more coherently ... can you write a novel?"
But I'm alone and I still dream so big yet live so small. Things will
change now. I feel it.

There is a switch in the air tonight. It's not suffocating, like breakups
all those years ago, but clean and clear. He does not want me anymore
so I tilt my head, take a breath and say, "Okay. I understand."

It's calm now. My heart didn't break, it kept on beating like a stoic
marching forward without looking back, and I will be a writer now.

I love so many people, still.
I think I will write about them forever.

Let it break so it can heal

I'm so sick of people writing inspirational posts about heartbreak. How it will grow you and teach you and time heals all wounds. I'm sick of it and I know I'm one of them. The everlasting hopeful writers who write pain into motivation to get a few likes and shares but fuck that. Heartbreak kills you. For a little while. You will heal and survive but it doesn't matter, it kills you for the moment. You're living in a static state of panic and stress, not knowing how to live or breathe or be and people keep telling you to just go on and "spend time with your friends" but to hell with that. You let it hurt because there's nothing else you can do. You let it hurt and burn and you live in a state of crying and fighting for weeks or months, until one day you just feel done. That is a thing, I promise. That day is a thing. That day you just feel done with this story. This same old sad imagination of what went wrong, what you could have done differently, how things could be. You're over it. You will be over it.

So I'm sorry people keep telling you to grow through a heartbreak, including me. You will just have to let it hurt, until you're done. Hurt until the hurt is done and one day you will just move on. That's all. That's your only job: hold on until the hurt is done.

That's all.

———————

Things will always linger. How you handled things, spoken or unspoken, left me wondering for days while you were out there making plans, making friends, making money.

I'm not sure you can stay friends with someone you used to love more than anything on this planet. I'm not sure you want to.

Love is the way

i'm bored
it's late
it's early
i'm drunk

i still feel the familiar feeling of being heartbroken but i no longer
have an object for the pain so i direct it towards myself and everyone i
meet. i'm heartbroken by people who pass me on the street, the dog
in the flat above, a line in a book or the way a dancer moves.
it's a quiet sunday. i cleaned my windows because ten years ago i was
convinced i had seasonal depression so i soak up natural daylight
when i can and feel heartbroken when i can't but i don't think i've
ever been depressed. only bored. under-stimulated. which is the
opposite of depression? i've only ever been too in love with life so i
feel heartbroken when i feel like life doesn't feel my love for it
which has happened a lot lately.

i don't love things enough. i love very little.
it's just one of many things i'm gonna change one day when things are
different.

when things are different i will set fire to my journals again and watch
the horizon from 9 different places before the year is over.
i think i might take someone with me this time.
i think the world will be kinder now.

Young writers

Young writers are doomed from the start.

We live and experience and turn our people into more exciting characters than they really are. Then we stop writing about them because the relationship gets stuck and now we live on habits. Now they wonder why we don't write.

Then love turns dark and we start writing a lot. To share. To help. Because is there anything that hurts more than love gone wrong when you're young? When you just want to be loved but are left unlovable? We want to write about it because it matters, and they all tell us to write about what matters. Sometimes in the past, during dark love, I managed to link those words together correctly and it clicked where it should click so the writing went viral and got shared everywhere and nowhere and people made me feel loved. They said: "thank you". They said: "keep writing". But then you fall in love again and that love feels sacred, only between you and two other eyes so you don't write about it. You don't want to share. He asks why you still write about dark love when his love is bright and you laugh it away, saying, "It's just fiction."

But then love—this new, bright love—turns dark again and you stay up until 5 a.m. letting your fingers run over the keyboard like they're telling a story of their own and suddenly it's real. It's not fiction.

So we write anyway, no matter what. We write the real, we write the unreal. We tweak and twist to make it a little more exciting or a little more painful. We write to share. Because someone else shared something that made us sit at 4 a.m. with wide-open eyes when the words hit like knives and we thanked the gods that someone took the time to write this. To help us. To let us know it's all okay.

I chase highs and lows in order to make my stories a little deeper. A little clearer. So you can understand. So you can say: "me too!" I'm studying storytelling and character development. To develop my character and live within my story. It's all the same now. I live my stories and they live me.

I will write until there's nothing left to write about and that day I will be finished.

Journal VIII

1. I know I should focus on my writing. I should write a "real" book.

2. I still want to be a songwriter.

3. I was most immersed in literature my first year in Berlin 2013–2014. I wrote two books in six months and wanted to be an author.

4. I keep using age as an excuse for everything. I'm too old to make it as an artist now. I'm too young to be a successful author. I'm too old to start a new relationship. I'm too young to fully commit.

5. I write so little when I feel strong and well.

6. I'm not yet used to not feeling devastated so I seek chaos and destruction.

Echoes

I'm here for you. Always. Do you feel me? Hear me? I talk to you
every night, does it reach you?
We could be close again, touching before violence, preparing each
other for a storm to come.
We both knew, always,
something wasn't right. The timing a little off. Spoke into each other,
over each other, never hearing always speaking.
But I'm with you, always.
So you live on the 6th floor with a view of the city. Bought wall art to
fill up your eyesight, a nice kitchen, inviting friends over every Friday.
I do too, almost. A basement, far away, it's lonely
but I'm with you
every night. Telling you things, saying
i'm sorry i'm sorry
do you hear it? Does it reach you?

Anyway. I kept saying "stay" while drifting further away but
I congratulate you on your new job! Qualifications and a new car!

i could still touch you.
relied on you
on the house
on the love
i still talk to you. i still touch you.

we could talk again like i talk to you all the time.

Lessons in Love Nr. 5

I can't write a book about love and how to make it last without bringing up the issue of me being a woman. Have you read the great Simone de Beauvoir's *The Second Sex*? If not, you should. It changed a lot for me. It's a complex existence and I take no side.

There is nothing more freeing than a mature woman who lives life on her own terms and goes where she pleases and is actively choosing no relationship, no children, no marriage. But the older I get, the more wisdom and strength I see in mature women who carry themselves with grace and elegance and still—still—have enough of themselves to share with a partner.

I can share myself with someone. No problem at all! I'm there for you no matter what and I'll come to you when you need me and I'll never ask for anything in return.

I leave myself to be there for someone else.

I'm also a lifelong professional at being independent without anyone or anything and I love it—setting fire to my tracks and moving wherever no one knows I'll go.

I do this masterfully, cut contact with everyone and everything and feel freer than the wind itself.

But how do you do both?

That's what you need though. You need both.

I want to be talked to like an intelligent human, but held like a woman.

I want to be respected like a strong individual, but loved like a woman.

I want to be treated like him, but met like a woman.

What does that make me?

Weak?

Or ... elegant?

Does it make me a traditionalist? Or a romantic?

I want him to buy me flowers and in return I want to give him my presence.

What does that make me?

03.00

suddenly the water glass on my table is making me sad.

i'm hungry. it's 3 a.m. i read someone else's book and thought of finishing my own but that won't make me happier. or?

it's still 3 a.m. and i'm still hungry and the water glass is still making me sad.

sometimes i call someone up from my past just to make me feel something. to remind myself that someone stepped out of my life because he didn't find it exciting here anymore and it's a great thing to do if you ever want to feel something. if you get bored of emotional stability. call someone up from your past and just talk a bit. chat about his new life with new exciting people, let him hang up without asking a question of you and then look at the lonely water glass on your table and remember that you're hungry and that it's 3 a.m. and you're still up alone.

it's 3 a.m. and everything is making me sad.

Anger

So those hands that now keep you safe at night will slowly let go and instead grasp elbows, not knowing where to look. Those eyes that now observe your every move, every little habit and every little quirk, will soon gaze down. That light you used to see behind them, somewhere inside that mind, will be replaced by a dark arrogance you can't fully read. You will try to reach through, with hands and words and touch and love but he will not answer. He will keep his head high. His voice will be tired. Uninterested. He will stop caring about your work. He won't stay up when you're coming home late. He will forget your anniversary, shrug his shoulders and say, "I'm sorry."

So this person that now keeps you safe will one day talk to you from behind a dark wall of something you cannot understand and you will stamp your feet for a while, for a year, until you give up. You will let your arms fall down, close your mouth, close your eyes, turn around and walk away.

It will happen again and again. It will happen again and again.

Lessons in Love Nr. 6

When I meet new people, I am always immediately intrigued by their lives. How do they live? What do they live for? What drives them? What baggage do they carry? How do they spend their days? I'd like to believe that I'm interested in these things because I'm a storyteller. I'm an artist and I'm writing about human interaction, human existence. And because I'm simply interested in other people. But I also see now that there is more behind this.

I've felt strong lately, but even on days when I feel strong and happy, excited about my future, I find myself holding on to people. Past relationships I can't let go of or temporary friendships I wish lasted longer. I've found myself feeling disconnected from people, like I can't really reach them, and I've tried to solve this by over-connecting, wanting to be there all the time. Know what they're doing, what they're thinking, what they're feeling. I turn obsessed with the idea of having those people around me and being close to them and I'm willing to go through anything to make them enjoy my company.

So this is what I've learned...

Because my own life has felt so empty and uninhabited, I've taken every opportunity I've found to "move in" to someone else's life. In every relationship I've had, I've moved into their lives. Leaving my own behind. I've taken on their routines and habits, interests and circle of friends because I've had none of my own. And when the relationship ends, I keep finding myself helpless and lonely, desperately trying to stand up on my own, because it's not just the person I lose—I also lose their life where I was living. I took it on like my own home, so I never know how to let go of people because I don't have a life of my own that feels full and warm enough to go back home to. I find myself homeless over and over again because I keep building my home in other people's lives.

I met someone that I so desperately wanted to invite into my life. Show him around. Take him to my places, my corners of the city, my daily routine and let him see how I live. But I stopped myself because I don't have a life I feel I can invite someone into. It's not full enough.

Now, I love my life. I love everything I have in it. But there is something about me trying so hard to live simply and with the bare minimum. I do things that usually go unnoticed and I create things that only my readers understand and then at the end of the day someone asks, "So what did you do today?" And I mumble, "Mmm, I wrote and created something and then I read some books and did some other things but whatever... What about you?" I don't think other people would find my days exciting so I try to hide them away, focus on others and avoid questions about myself.

You know those people you meet who just feel safe? They radiate certainty and belonging, like everything will be okay for them, because they know how to make things okay. If you're lucky enough to spend a day with them they will go on with their lives and let you be a tourist in there. They make each moment their own, in small ways, like having preferences about the music, the colors, the smells, the direction, the order of things. And they will talk about their lives in a way that doesn't leave any space for questioning. It's not like ... *hello, this is my life, do you think it's okay?* Like I do ... It's more like: "Hey, this is my life! It's nice, isn't it? Now show me yours!"

So I took a trip to the other side of the planet and moved into my friend's life for 2 weeks. A little house in LA, daily plans, a car, events to attend, people to see. And every night I fell asleep feeling both proud of him for having created that life for himself, but also with a new realization of why I feel so lost and lonely: I need to build out my life. I need to build it to the point of no longer feeling the need to move out of it. I must build my home in my own life. And it sounds so silly and so simple but if you get it you get it, and then it's the most profound thought ever.

So, how do you do that? How do you build a life that feels full? A life you don't want to move out of as soon as you meet someone else with an interesting life? So that, when you do meet someone with an interesting life, you will have one too, and you'll be two complete individuals, who can invite each other into each other's lives, but you'll both feel at home and secure knowing that your life won't be lost. You stand strong and sure in your own and so will he, or she. That's a healthy relationship. To yourself and to someone else.

Sometimes you need to go to the other side of the planet to see the bigger picture of things. I think that's what my trip to LA did for me. Now I know I must start living my life for myself and fill it with all things beautiful so I no longer want to move out of it. Maybe even make it so pretty that someone might want to move into it one day? I'm up for the challenge.

Journal IX

I'm taking the first morning bus to catch whatever there is to catch.

I never let the alarm clock ring, I'm already up; already awake. My eyes never rest heavy for more than a minute or two and my senses are sharp. Alert.

I learned to escape my dark mind by simply not going there, not staying up that long, and when I do find myself still awake in the early hours I make use of it.

But the morning hours hold a clarity so clear and pure that nothing can disturb my peace of mind and heart. I walk surer, taller, quieter. I don't speak often but if I did I would know what to say but still explore the terrain like a traveler on new land. I would find new words to explain my inward thoughts and I would not be ashamed. Of my language. Of my accent. Of the way I choose to explain myself.

Memories from years ago keep flashing up before my eyes, on the internet, on the digital devices I never wanted to have but still hold and it's like something or someone wants to give subtle hints and say: "Hey, look how far you've come! This was you three years ago! And this was five years ago! Look where you are right now, isn't it magical?!"

It gets to me. I tend to just go on and judge my improvements with the eyes of a critic. Every birthday screaming, "I SHOULD BE SO MUCH MORE BY NOW!" But then you let the years go by and you do the best you can and after a while you throw your glance in the rearview and realize *huh, it led me somewhere.* All these small steps each and every day. They add up. Just do the best you can, moment by moment.

4 a.m. and I've never been so awake. Who knew this was where I'd find my space.

The sky is busy tonight

Before you became my friend
I sat by the front porch every morning watching mums drag their
kids to school
and teenagers drag their feet
and I grasped my coffee cup tightly to my chest as if it was something
to hold on to
and some days the postman came early and said good morning,
walked all the way onto my lawn to give me the newspaper, with a
smile,
jealous because I was sitting on the front porch, not going to work.

Before you became my friend
I stretched the nights until they became mornings.
I kept the light on, fell asleep on the sofa, not using my bed,
and my house was always clean, nothing unnecessary owned or
belonged
and I kept the same necklace on forever
as I remember it.
because it meant something.

I've lied my way to forgiveness from people who wouldn't really care
about the lie, but it felt better. The priests and gurus have a steady
hand, a firm gaze straight into my eyes. I'm always there alone, they
wonder why but can't ask. One wise man in his elder years wore a
robe and practiced meditation like his only destiny was to be silent
but he had a laugh that made his whole body shake with passion and
it echoed all over that place, where we sat, on the floor, looking for
salvation.

No one seeks salvation unless they need it. No one starts praying in
the midst of a life or reads philosophy or tries to understand Seneca

unless they need it. We go there looking for help, looking for answers, hoping someone can save us from ourselves, mostly, maybe someone else, but happy people are happy and not concerned with going silent. I sat on that floor with a heart of stone, no emotions to be felt and I grew like a rock. Hard and cold, steady-rooted to the bottom of the sea and I tried all kinds of chemicals to clip those roots off but they left me floating, away and off, so I came back. I heard speeches on forgiveness, on loving all and all around, repeating every word like scripture in my head. I kept sitting there, even after I left, gazing emptily inside my mind, eyes closed, or maybe open, I can't remember.

I used to travel on trains with books and songs, prepared to make the journey something like the scene of a movie. I wrote and smiled and looked out now and then, pretending it was never-ending.

Now I pick my feet up from the platform, trying to take no space. I sit down where the seat is free and spend 4 hours gazing out the window. Not a thought. Not a view. Not one single feeling to feel or hold on to. It's all gone away. Years of living wears you out. But it also makes you softer. Kinder. Easier to bend and things no longer get to you, as much at least. He screamed straight into my ear, telling me to wake up,

to say something,

to show any sign of aliveness

but I had no interest in showing anything at all

so I simply smiled and said, "I think I'll go now"

and then I left and it didn't get to me.

I used to wake up early, 6 a.m., free and awake. I liked the purity, the clean streets, the crisp air. I liked the silence, the way I saw the world come alive slowly, feeling like I was ahead of it.

Now I move with the moon. I greet the half-moon like a guru and the full moon is a pact with the sky, to make things last this time. I put my right hand on my chest and throw a spell off to the gods, or the moon, or whoever is there, really, and it makes me feel holy, like I'm not a part of the rest but just this, the bigger. Part of something bigger. Like I have my own tale to tell and to walk and I don't have to say a thing. I don't have to speak. Or feel. I just go on and live with the moon.

There was a man working at the graveyard I pass by some nights and he looked so kind I felt like sitting down on that bench next to him, just watching him work.

I'm done with the noises, the loud screams for help. I am settled into silence and I know secrets no one told me and I can share them with whoever wants to listen.

The sky is busy tonight. I wonder who's under it more than me?

Everything goes back to him

You got this one person and everything goes back to him. You eat and unconsciously compare it to the dinners he used to cook for you. The excitement in his eyes when he tried out something new and wanted you to be just as excited.

You go swimming and think about the time you went to Spain. Morning swims with the sunrise, the sun reflecting in his eyes.

Everything goes back to him.

Then you grow older. Years go by. Relationships come and go. You fall in love, fall out of love, move on and move away. You find yourself 20 years older, go to the cinema and out of nowhere you order a small popcorn and suddenly hear him telling you to get a big one because life is short and we deserve it.

People don't leave you. You can get over them and move on. You keep writing the script of your life, but people don't leave you. The memory of everyone you ever met belongs to you and they become a part of you. Your character is made up of everyone you ever opened up to, and who opened up to you.

You got this one person and everything goes back to him. People don't leave you. They become a part of you.

Journal X

We kept in touch for 14 months. Every day, like always. A morning message, asking how the days were, the weather, the work, the music. Nothing changed. Maybe he was scared to be alone. Maybe he wasn't really sure yet. But hold on he did, without ever holding on, just not letting me go.

They don't even know about you

I look for words for a second or ten and end up asking about
names and hobbies, things that say nothing.
I nod my head and sip my drink and try to keep my senses still
when all I really want to tell them about
is you.

Free-floating leaf

Bali, 2019

I only breathe in fully in rare moments of walking home barefoot at midnight. Slowly, wearing a simple t-shirt, no make-up, salt in my hair. It's summer. It's warm. I dream, I wander and I have rare moments of endless nights where I breathe in fully.

I tiptoe on the street lines, like a ballerina, and he's carrying my shoes. I share, I listen, I laugh freely straight out into the night and he smiles —at me laughing, maybe. I don't think of fame or glory, money or contracts. I don't think of other years, past or future, the mornings in the hallways, wanting someone to stay. anyone.

I think nothing of that, I only think of this sky, this moment, this night. His voice sounding strange and unfamiliar and he has a weird way of turning his whole body towards me when I'm talking, like he wants to take it all in, not just listen—he wants to see it all. We say goodbye and I walk the last bit alone, feeling better. feeling lighter.

I'm still a free-floating leaf in the universe, going places on my own without telling anyone about my plans. I pack my things, board that plane and off I go. I sleep alone, I wake alone, but I have moments of speeding through empty streets at midnight, or walking home with someone who sounds strange and wonderful, telling stories until the sun comes up, and I breathe in fully, wanting to stay a little longer, just another breath.

If I close my eyes I'm still walking on that street with the stars above me.

Letting go

It was the most liberating thing, deciding to let things just be as they are. Driving off, leaving things behind. The clarity that appeared the second I decided to stop trying to change yesterday. I can't save situations that are already broken. I can't unsay things or unmeet people. I saw that my only choice is to either unwillingly move forward with anger and regrets about the past, or simply accept how things unfolded, let them go, completely, and move forward with no grudges.

This relationship didn't work out ... I will spend no more time wondering what I could have done differently and instead accept an ending, and just let it be. This plan did not go accordingly ... I won't waste another second feeling low because I failed. I will leave it here, completely, and instead look forward to a new plan.

From now on, I will get so consumed with my future that I won't have any time to feel sad about the past. I will feel so excited about the clear path in front of me, that I won't have any space left to feel devastated about yesterday.

Don't bring heavy regrets with you as you journey forward. Forgive people and let them be. Forgive places and simply leave. Free yourself, let things go. Imagine a future where you hold no grudges towards anyone. You're not angry at past lovers, not bitter about failures, not disappointed in your parents. You forgive, send love and move on. You're free.

It is the most liberating thing, to just let things be as they are.

He loved me some days. I'm sure he did.

BACK TO BERLIN

2019

Growing up as an artist

You know, it's quite different being an artist at 18 and 28.

You're 18 and everything is intense and loud and magical and it all gets to you so no drugs are needed. You write from an ecstatic state of euphoria, trying to catch the feelings before they flee.

Then you're 23 and you're chasing the same euphoria but things are harder to catch now. You've grown thicker skin; things don't get to you as easily. You inhale whatever you get your hands on because art needs to be rooted in something and somehow you feel fleeting. Sinking. You haven't yet found your place in this world so you seek people or bodies or drugs to feel something.

And now?

It's different now.

Feelings don't flee. They almost don't come at all. It's a systematic allowance. What makes sense to my intellect?

intellect...

Intellect killed my artistic endeavor: i'm too smart to suffer now. i know how to think myself happy, abandoned the sorrows of young Werther to spend the nights with neuroscientists. i decided they know better. but knowing better is not always better because i had fun back then, wrote with fire and passion. now i'm calculating every word, every line, thinking before i type.

So now there is no sorrow, only psychology and brain wiring and it's honestly the most boring choice i've ever made because I miss the ecstasy of pain and happiness.

I miss staying up until 3 a.m. writing myself alive, finding people and places to fit my stories.

On the outside

I'm trying so hard to make myself a part of something, be one of anything, belong to this or that, people and this city

but no matter how much I reach out or make an effort I still stand on the outside. I'm not a part of it. I can't integrate myself into people or communities, walking on the outside, looking in.

There is still a piece of glass between me and the world that I so badly want to be a part of but I can't find an opening. I put my hands on the glass wanting someone to let me in but they just smile, a polite nod, inviting me to have a seat, sitting on the other side, looking in.

I want so badly to be the person people go to. I want so badly to be the one they call when they need to talk or laugh or cry or do anything at all

and I go out of my way to be of service. I go wherever they are at any time, smile and move out of the way and try the best I can to be useful

but I'm on the outside. I can't get in.

There is still a piece of glass between me and the world and all I want is to be in there.

Berlin is lovely. Lonely but lovely.

The impossibility of someone loving you

It's the impossibility of someone loving you.

It's the unimaginable thought that someone finds you exciting and safe at the same time.

It's the incomprehensible idea that you're not annoying. You're not small. You're not in the way of anyone or anything and it's the slight chance that someone really wants you there, next to him. Finds you intelligent, even. Wants to learn your thoughts and ways, because to someone you're inspiring.

He finds you inspiring.

You make a few rounds and you learn to apologize. Say: "I'm sorry," before you really know what you've done wrong but he looks angry so you look down at your feet, feeling stupid, feeling clumsy. You want to ask if you should just leave, to make it easier for him, so he doesn't have to deal with you anymore, this cold-hearted person who's so hard to love.

That's what he makes you feel like.

Like you're hard to love. Like you're cold, mean, not a good person but then there's someone else telling you you're inspiring. You're special. He likes everything about you and you find yourself saying, "I'm sorry," but he just giggles and says, "What for?!" and he makes you feel like you're taking the lead. Like you're ahead and he's happy to get to be with you.

He makes you feel like you're doing things right. Like you're good. You're a good person.

So how do you unlearn the learned behavior of apologizing for being yourself? Because someone made you feel like you shouldn't be here. You're not welcomed. You're wrong. You know nothing. How do you accept that the impossible thought of someone truly loving you is completely possible? And how do you accept that love? How do you nurture it? How do you love back, when the love you tried to give was rejected and you stopped giving it out? How do you learn to give it out again?

Moving on

You know you've moved on when you find other people beautiful.
When you don't avert your eyes but keep them steady
or when you stay the night, the last one at the party,
and you don't feel sorry. or empty. or guilty
because whatever, where are you going anyway?

i used to sit here, in this same pub in this same city
7 years ago, writing another book,
like i am now
again
and i wrote myself out of heartbreak with that book
like i am now
i guess.
in some ways maybe i've written myself into heartbreak this time but
i'm coming out of it.
at least i find other people beautiful again. they make me smile.
maybe more than i have before and i have a good feeling about
things.

You know you've moved on when you find other people beautiful.

The truth

I'm about to piss off a lot of people right now. The truth usually does that.

80% of people's complaints are about situations that can be changed in one day.

The other 20% are about real complaints that can't be changed, and then what does complaining about it do?

So you're unhappy about the situation you're in? Change it. Now. Cut the ropes. Don't text her back. Change your job. Learn a new skill. Sell your house and move to a new city. Start over. Get healthy, start running. Or play tennis. Or anything that gets you moving. Cut out processed food. Cut out sugar.

Read books. Listen to audiobooks. Or watch YouTube videos.

You live in a time where there are zero excuses. You can do anything you want! You want a new life? Well, you can have it? But no one will hand it to you on a silver plate, you will have to stand up from that couch and go get it yourself. Because no one else cares. No one cares about how you live your life but you.

That's the downside of this time and age: you're on your own. But don't you dare run and complain about it to me because I'm the loneliest of you all! No one is as lonely as me! I have no one and nothing and I've lived my life completely by myself and I'm so terribly lonely you don't even know where in the world I am!

See? See that?

We all do it. We all build identities around our problems. Why do we do that? Why do we choose to identify with our problems? I've spent the last few years feeling a little lonely but still I wake up each day reminding myself of how lonely I am even though I'm not lonely anymore. Why do I take pride in my loneliness? Why do I keep talking about it? Writing about it? Reminding myself about it?

Because who am I without it? Who am I without feeling lonely? It's a feeling that has occupied my inner space for so many years that if I let it go it will be empty space. What do I fill it with?

So you miss someone who left? By choice or not by choice. You're angry because your parents did you wrong. You're devastated because you got laid off and now you're left with a house and no income.
That second you spent complaining about it you could have spent finding a new job. Or reading about grief processing. Or going for a run.

I do it too. I complain and I keep talking about it when really all I need to do is make a change.

No more complaining. No more crying about situations that can be changed. From now on I will only tell people about how much progress I'm making.

A dark forest not to enter

I'm becoming more and more aware of how each individual makes me feel. Which direction they throw me in, what thoughts I go to sleep with after spending an evening with them.

We have the fun ones. The ones that you go for too many drinks with and laugh and talk about absolutely nothing with and you go home feeling like you really didn't experience anything new but you had fun and laughed a lot and that's great.

You won't call them at 2 a.m. when you panic and don't know where to go even though you know they'd offer you their couch.

We have the very kind ones. The soft and open ones. They hug you like they've known you forever and truly like you and they say your name often and always text you back within 5 minutes. You walk home after a hang in the park feeling warm and soft and kind, but you won't think about them tomorrow.

They would up and leave whatever they were doing at 2 a.m. to come sit with you on the floor.

Then there are the darkly attractive ones, for one reason or another. This is where it gets complicated. Twisted like a delicious psychological horror movie you're thankful to only be watching and not live in but still you love watching it.

That rare person who makes you open your eyes a little wider and for a brief instant you don't think about the bills and the rent — all you see is him.

I'm attracted to people's intellect. I'm attracted to someone's way of speaking. Their life choices or how they think about success.

The way he looks everyone straight in the eyes when he's waiting for their answer, like for a split second he gives them his undivided attention, and I can't stop witnessing it.

It might have been the way he shook my hand, a bit too firmly and I was stuck. I want to know all about him and always be near.

I walk home feeling neither warm, nor soft, and I did not laugh a lot. I'm ... anxious? Is that anxiety? I go to sleep feeling ... sad? Full of sadness. Lying in a pool full of sadness and anxious worrying. But I enjoyed it? I loved it, even? I want to know all about him and I need him to find me magical.

I care what he thinks about me. I'm not one of those intriguing people. I'm open and sharp and ask too many questions way too fast, or just stay quiet for 10 hours straight because I like to observe, sometimes,

but I'm not attractively intriguing.

I can't sleep.

The next morning the kind and soft and fun people will be out of my sphere: all I think about is him and I wonder if he'll text, if I should text, if he's as dark and depressed as I think. He was immature at times. I didn't want him to feel so, but also didn't want him to feel too much better than me so I put him in his place sometimes. I regret it.

I can't stop thinking about the way he felt arrogant and loving at the same time. How did he do that? And he made me feel small and insignificant and like I said very stupid things but still I text him. He does not text back. 3 days. 4 days. "Sorry, your message slipped, maybe next week, okay?"

I will text him next week.

He's like a dark forest I can't help but enter.

I am so happy not being in love

I woke up sweating because i dreamt my face was on a big billboard somewhere important, promoting something i created, and it was awful and greedy and sold really really well and i knew it was a dream because i saw the billboard from the seat of my car, driving, and i don't drive
in real life
so i knew it was a dream
but also because i was on a billboard
and because i didn't like it.

I forget about everyone i swore i'd never forget
and keep thinking about people i want nothing more than to not remember
anymore.

for a while when i was younger i had this breathing tic where i thought i didn't get enough air in a normal breath so i forced myself to keep going with the inhale like i was gasping for air. my teacher thought i had asthma and sent me to the doctor but no, i said, i just need to breathe in a bit more than everyone else. nothing strange at all.
lately i've felt the same feeling of not getting enough air, like my lungs are not big enough. so i inhale inhale inhale until my lungs are about to explode and it still feels like i'm not getting enough air so i breathe until i get dizzy and have to lie down.
i know it's just a tic but i also think my mind has some sort of asthma but i'm not sure how to treat it.

i am so happy not being in love.
i don't think i ever want to be in love
again.

Would I change if I could?

May. Thursday. I picked the fancy coffee shop over the cheap one, because I'm tired of decadence. I'm tired of worn-out clothes. Worn-out shoes. Hiding in the train toilet to get to a new town.

Would I change, if I could? Would I pick up the stride from the ground and fight my way into new armor? I am not sure.
There is a romanticized story about girls who leave and wander; throwing caution to the wind. People think we're happy with ourselves. That we can speak freely and surely with anyone about anything. The horizon from a new bridge in a new town; conversations with foreign accents; new smells in new coffee shops.

Would I change, if I could? Would I fight my way into existence, away from this corner I'm living out my life in? I am not sure.

I have rooted myself in this quiet place where I don't need much to get by. I need my visions. I need my books. I need new thoughts and lessons, from older souls, bars, whisky, libraries; different ones in different towns. I need my music. I need my songs. I need the safety of somewhere to rest my head at night when my eyes get heavy. And I need space. Lots of space. To run, sing, and change around in any way I please—outer or inner—and I need to love. I need the space to love ideas and pieces, anywhere I can find, and I need the peace of mind to understand them. A letter, from a stranger, from a melody written right on time, by me or anyone else.

It's December. It's Tuesday. I'm drinking coffee from a polished cup, and the rain washes the streets clean. Would I change, if I could?

I am slowly coming to the conclusion that it's more important to learn to work with what you've got, under the circumstances you've been given, than wishing for different ones.

Attractively meaningless

I'm tired of being an ignorant asshole who doesn't care about saving the planet.

i only want to save myself.

be the only one left in this rotten place

only it won't be rotten anymore

it will be me and the flowers, blooming lovelier than ever before

and i will build a treehouse by the ocean. learn how to like being in the water

not just look at it

swim every morning. befriend the earth and the sky

and lately i've been thinking: loneliness only haunts me when i have the choice to not choose it. loneliness hurts because it's a choice. because there are people out there, outside the window, no matter where in the world i am, there are people outside but i choose to look down when someone smiles at me so i feel lonely.

but if i had no choice, let's say, if one day the big people said: "the earth is closed, go home, stay inside, see no one" loneliness wouldn't be a choice and it wouldn't feel lonely?

maybe?

anyway, i'm sick of not caring about saving the planet

i just want to save myself

and some trees

the ocean

it would be lovely and quiet and awfully terrifyingly attractively meaningless.

Journal XI

July, 2020

1. I have finally settled into my work. I wake up early, greet the sun and set pen to paper. This is simple happiness.

2. I walk the streets when I can't sleep, or don't want to, 'cause this city has never felt more alive and calm at the same time and I've never loved it more than I do now. Some nights I lay down on the football field, remembering younger days when I used to sleep wherever I could rest my head because rent was a privilege I couldn't afford and I just wanted to be a writer.

3. It seems the more I embrace my profession the more interesting people I attract. I've walked home after midnight every night this week, feeling satisfied from good conversations. I've missed it. The calmness after feeling like someone saw something good in me. I didn't feel it for so very long, but now I do.

4. I think I will sleep better when I write better, but I'm not sure what must come first.

5. Some nights I pack all essentials in a rucksack and climb up a little stairway near the fire station. I still crave watching cities from above, but I no longer close my eyes and imagine jumping.

6. It's none of my business what people think of my art. My only job is to create it.

Your people

I spent the majority of my 20s feeling embarrassed about my own life and character. I surrounded myself with people who made me feel small and unimportant, like I was always in their way, never contributing anything but burdens and negativity. Then at some point last year I pulled myself out of that storyline I wrote for myself and fought to write a new storyline. A new narrative.

You never realize how much your closest people influence who you think you are until you spend time with someone who thinks you're a great person. Someone who values your opinions, listens to you like you have important things to share, wisdom and knowledge. Someone who finds you genuine and funny, strong and independent. And you see how someone's belief that you are those things makes you take them on and find them in yourself and suddenly you see how all those other years you took on the character of someone else because those other people kept repeating it to you, like a mantra...

"you're too much. you're nothing without me. you don't understand. i don't have time for you. you're too lonely and and and …"

but that's not you. that's someone else's idea of you. without other people's ideas of who you are … there is you. and you can be whoever you want to be.

so surround yourself with people who see the good in you, so you can see it too. surround yourself with people who talk about you like you're doing some great in the world. like they're proud to know you. and see how you slowly relax those shoulders, stand a little straighter, and maybe by the end of a long, long ride find yourself feeling proud to know yourself, too, and what you've been through and what you learned from it.

from now on i will only be around people who want to see the good in me. and i will resolve to see the good in others and help them see it too.

that's where really beautiful things happen.

Journal XII

1. i packed a bag and went to Sweden. i need it now. open space, landscape, clean air. it seems like no one informed people in Sweden about a pandemic raging the planet, but we also have a built-in fear of being too close to other people here so it might just add up. i don't know though.

2. it took me 30 years to feel close to myself and i blame that on Sweden. it's not Sweden's fault, obviously, but i still think it happened because i grew up here and it feels good to blame someone, or something. took me 30 years to build an intimate, caring relationship to my body and mind, my life and my future but still i can't remember seeing any adults around me who truly cared for themselves when i was younger so how could i have known?
my first relationship was a disaster and i loved it. why?
someone i truly loved wanted to have a family with me and i told him my parents didn't fight a lot but i don't think they truly loved each other until all their kids had moved out. ask me again if i want kids?

3. i've been a hectic person—"high blood pressure", they told me—since i was 12 years old. i blamed it on me trying not to eat 'cause after 3 days my heart was racing quite well. but i also said not eating made me feel calm so it didn't really match up. i didn't want to think more about it.

4. i work with a woman who teaches me about the 'sacred feminine' and she keeps telling me, "you're so masculine! you're too hard! soften, charlotte, soften." and i didn't understand what she meant
but now i do.

5. i met someone who said he needed to feel that he could take care of me, but that he felt like he could never take care of me as well as i

take care of myself and i've never felt more proud of myself than i did in that moment.

Go back and make things right

Okay so listen...

I've written four books about leaving, songs and poems, had an endless romance with starting over, packing light.

But have you ever tried returning? Have you tried going back to make things right?

Have you ever left a city small and sad, determined to never return but then you're out there for a few years, roaming the streets, intertwining with people. You make a few rounds, collect some hearts, some wounds, and one day you come to one of those lakes where everything is still and quiet. The clouds are reflecting on the surface and it's like you see your own thoughts and past and habitual ways in the sky, everywhere, telling you something. This lake can be real or not, either way, this is what it feels like. You run and run and run and run and suddenly there's a still lake reflecting clouds on the surface. You sit down, because lakes like these tell you to do so, and you sit there for a while, tilting your head, seeing your own ways from different angles.

Maybe that tragedy wasn't so tragic after all? Maybe that boy just tried to go on well? Maybe this loneliness isn't so terrible to live with as long as you know that you can meet new people any second of any day your whole life through. You can still reach out; you're not an island.

You find yourself letting go of all the stories you've held on to, things that happened in these cities, people they belonged to, and now you go back...

I've spent the first part of my life leaving places and people and versions of myself, but lately, I've started returning. I go back to all the places I once left. I left them angry and sad, broken and small.

Usually disappointed in people and situations. I have one person for each city I've ever lived in, and I kept thinking I could never go back because that city belonged to us, how we were then, and I thought I had to leave and never return in order to move on and get over.

But that's not wisdom. That's not growth. That's limitation and giving a piece of the world to someone you think acted wrong.

So maybe that's what true moving on looks like: learning that nothing is ever attached to something physical. No emotion or heartbreak or catastrophic escape is ever attached to a city or a person or a house: it's all in you. And you can change. You can move on. You can twist and turn around, take a new shape and let go.

So try to go back. Go back to that corner of that city where that man broke your heart, looked you in the eyes and told you that he just does not love you anymore. Stand there and imagine that younger you, trying to keep her head up, trying not to choke on that stone in her throat. Imagine placing a hand on her shoulder, as if saying: "Just keep breathing, you'll be okay." Imagine saying: "You'll come back here in 7 years, standing strong and tall, thinking back on that relationship, seeing how it was a teenage love. Seeing how that person wouldn't be a fit for you now, being older, being wiser, being different."

Go back to that corner and stand there for a few seconds, breathe it in, look at your hands: older, wiser. Now take that corner back. Take it back! Make it yours. Create a new feeling there, from this calmer state of stability you're in now.

Now drop the story: what does this city look like without the heartbreak story?

Pretty nice, huh? The sun is shining. The people are laughing. You buy yourself a drink and observe the youth writing at the table across the room. You used to be her, but not anymore. You watch her hitting those keys frantically, trying to capture a story before it disappears and you smile, sipping your drink, knowing you did the same. 7 years ago. But not anymore.

You think before you write now. You consider different angles, different tones, different points of view. Then you write, like a "real" writer, tweaking and correcting, thinking about it strategically.

There is a time for leaving and moving on, but there should also be a time for returning. Taking back what once was yours. Berlin isn't his; it's whatever I make of it. It's mine. Bristol isn't what happened that night or those early mornings crying by the water; I can go there and make it something new, now.

The city I grew up in isn't lost to teenage me, angry and sad; I can make it new—I can make it mine again.

Go back and make things right. Don't reach the end of your life with a world full of places you've left and can't go back to. End it with a world full of places you love, nothing but beautiful memories that erase the dark ones. Take ownership of your own memories.

Take ownership of your world. Go back and make things right.

I'm too busy thinking about living

There are certain songs that always make me want to write. I'm sitting on the bus, in the car, at the bar and that song comes on and the stories just crystallize themselves in my chest. It feels like they start there, somewhere in my heart, and slowly grow outwards, and they need to go somewhere so I must write them down and I just let my fingers run until they have written themselves and there they are. I take a breath, like, relieved I got it down. That feels good. That always feels good.

So I don't write a lot anymore. I work in silence. Trying to stay focused. "Deep work" some high-profiled author called it. And I'm sick and tired of them all. "Authors" who don't write their own books. Marketing experts using clickbait and multi-million-dollar PR budgets to get their "art" seen and heard.
Maybe I'm just jealous. Probably I'm just jealous.
I want it too. I want it all. The multi-million-dollar PR budget and all things glory.

But I'm also happy just doing me. Being me. Writing sometimes— when this song comes on, then I write, always. Times have changed. I'm older. I feel so much older. I laugh sometimes but mostly I work. I write and plan, strategically outline my days so no minutes go missing.

I don't think about dying anymore. I don't think about death.
That's the most profound thing I can ever share.
I don't think about dying anymore, I'm too busy thinking about living.
That's the most profound thing I will ever write.

New beginning

You made space in the bathroom for things I might need after just one night together because that's you and that's how you do things. But I spent 6 years with my ex and never really knew if he was happy or if he was leaving

or if I was

and I had to ask permission to stay over, apologizing no matter what and my friends never met him 'cause he was always busy

because that was him

but this is you.

Known you for 8 days and now you're making space in the bathroom so I feel welcomed. "You can stay over?" "My home is your home." Smiling, a hand above your heart, me thinking

I grew so much older so quickly from all that happened,

all of all of that.

And he feels so light, shoulders relaxed

but still older than me, already past this, on the other side.

"Just give me some time," I keep saying, "ease into it." But he's already in the kitchen making plans of where we can go together

and I sit on the bed thinking there were so many places I wanted to go to with the last one but never did because he was too busy, not excited, tired?

But this is it now, not that or them or those but him, in the kitchen, making plans, making breakfast, looking at me like I'm something to look at.

Maybe, if I learn to care more about the moment I'm in rather than how it might end, this could be it? A lovely collection of moments I might not want to end.

Life

i drink coffee and pay my bills, then i drink some over-priced drink in a noisy bar, and i spend time with people but never feel like i know them and suddenly i tell the world i'm writing a book and i haven't written in months. i fall in love with someone who does not fall in love with me and then i work on myself a little more until i throw my fist in the air stating "i'm complete on my own!" and then i drink a little more and write a little more and sleep a little less and then i fall in love with someone who does not fall in love with me, or the other way around, and we go drinking over-priced drinks in noisy places and i hold his hand a little tighter and try not to say i love him. then i get a little lost and only write texts around 3am and then i wake up next to someone but wish i was alone. then I wake up alone but wish I was next to someone. so i go drinking and find someone to fall in love with and hold his hand a little tighter and then i say "i'm gonna write a book!" and he finds that exciting and calls me patti smith and says i drink a bit too much and then he goes to work and then he saves a lot of money and then he wants to go on holiday and i say "writers don't go on holiday" and he smiles but doesn't find it funny and then i put that in a book and he never mentions it but at least i'm a writer and he likes that.

Complete healing

I hired a life coach because I was skeptical about life and basically just needed someone to coach me in how to live. So I found a life coach and she didn't ask me how I felt, like my therapist did for twenty-plus years. Instead she asked me, "How is future you?" I burst out laughing, like, it was a joke, right? "How is future you?" she said again, big smile, annoyingly white teeth, shiny hair, waiting for my answer.

See, my life coach doesn't care about past me or now me, only future me and how we can care for her and that's why I love her, my life coach. She cares, but only about future me.

So we've cared for future me for a few months now and I feel really good about her. Feel both good about her, as in my life coach and in her, future me. Apparently, I use the words 'peaceful' and 'content' a lot and my life coach keeps saying, "Aim higher! Want more!!" and I try really hard, stare at the white wall for 10 minutes as if I can find my 'something more' in there but all I keep wanting is ... "To feel peaceful. And calm. Yeah, that's all I want. No more sad."

My life coach tells me it's okay, future me is a work in progress and we'll get there. A supportive smile.

Today I understood complete healing.

Healing is not when you don't feel sad anymore. Healing is not when you're no longer crying every evening at 11 p.m. Healing is not when you'll be happy just feeling 'peaceful', or 'content'.

Healing is when you've moved beyond settling for peaceful and content and want more again. Healing is when you're back to wanting it all. The whole world or nothing.

I called my life coach and said: "I want more now! I want more!" and I told her about a beautiful apartment with large windows, a balcony and a view of the city. A dog, a book deal, a healthy body; a bookshelf with hundreds of books and friends! Great friends! Loving friends! Friends that come over for coffee on Sunday mornings because they know they're always invited. A driving license, a car, road trips in Portugal! Italy! California!

I told her about all the dreams I have and she said, "Stop calling them dreams," and I said "OKAY!" and I went to sleep and slept better than I have in 29 years.

It's okay to want more, you know? It's okay to not feel satisfied with just being okay. Go for amazing! Go for really f**king successful!

My life coach told me all this was possible, and I laughed a bit again, like when she first asked about future me, but this time I knew she was serious, and maybe next week I won't even laugh but just start planning, and maybe in a few weeks after that I'll even believe my dreams are not dreams but plans and wouldn't that be grand?

It's great, having someone coaching you in life. You should try it. Dare to aim higher.

The year I changed my own character

The year I changed my own character.
The year I stopped fleeing.
The year I took responsibility for my own becoming.
For my own happening. For my own success and happiness, home and surroundings.
The year I learned how to quit being myself, and instead design a new self, deliberately, consciously, maturely.

The year my heart broke, quietly dying. The year the vision I've had for a peaceful future was erased and gone, the house I thought I was living in was thrown up in the air during the calmest summer day, and I waved my arms screaming for someone to save me.
This was the year I learned to depend on myself. On my own ability to get by, even when I think I can't, and this was the year I became my own savior. The year I built my own home. From the ground up. A foundation to stand on. A stronger character. A loving heart.

Because when a heart gets broken, it's wide open.

When a heart gets broken, it's wide open to take in and give out. To learn and to grow, stronger and wiser, and an open heart is a brave heart because it can feel and hear and see it all. An open heart is a brave heart, because it knows there's no turning back. Only bravely facing forward, one foot in front of the other, slowly moving on to something better, something new.

This was the year I went to sleep some nights thinking, I'm done. Feeling finished. I had a good life. I learned a lot. the year I understood surrender. The desperate feeling of no longer wanting to be here, anyone, anymore, again. alone. alone. alone.

This was the year I sat down and faced the sky and screamed out with my arms wide open saying, "I just want to rest! In peace, in quiet, in assuring knowledge that all will be well."

But no one will come and save you. No one will take your hand and guide you to a better life. You must create it yourself. You must collect your mentors, dead or alive, and you must accumulate wisdom and knowledge, visions and goals.
You must decide what you want with your life. You must decide who you are trying to be.

This was the year I learned to no longer depend on other people to get by, nor be stubbornly independent without any help from anyone or anything.
This was the year I instead learned to say: you can depend on me. I will be your stability, you can always count on me.
I said it to myself and to others, over and over until I believed it. I will stand like a lighthouse in the storm and repeat over and over
you can depend on me.

This was the year I stopped begging for things to happen, and instead made them happen myself. This was the year I stopped living my life according to someone else's needs, and instead explored my own.
This was the year I learned to stop begging people to love me. If someone wants to go, let them go. This was the year I learned that every person who shows up in your life is there to teach you a lesson, and they will stay until you have learned what you need to learn. Then they will leave, whether you want them to or not, and you must let them. This was the year I learned that you must dare to leave something or someone completely, leaving that space empty and aching, in order to open up space for something new. And you must know that there is a new lesson and a new person, in a new place with a new life waiting for you.

This was the year I learned that what's coming is always better than what has been.

Don't hold on to things that are over. Let them go, bravely.

How to leave someone

Epilogue

It is the hardest thing in the world to tell someone you still love to exit your life.

How do you do it? Where is the BuzzFeed article on how to kindly tell someone to never again write to you? Never again send photos of his friends, his family, his holiday in Portugal?

Why does he do it in the first place? Why do people tell you they no longer want to be a part of your life, then can't let go? They hold on, with one hand, while also moving on but making sure you don't. Just in case they change their minds.

Don't be like that. You. Don't be like that person.
Be bigger. Be more sophisticated. Be a class act.
Respect other people. Make a decision. Want them in your life or don't want them in your life.
If you leave someone, do everything for them to be happy again. Make it easy for them to move on. Be happy when they meet someone new. Be happy when they stop reading your messages. Be happy when she stops replying. It means she found a way to live with the emptiness you caused and it means she found a way to be happy without you.
Be happy about that.
Be a class act.

I wrote a book three years ago about feeling lonely within love. I was proud of it and the poems were real. They hurt to write and they hurt to read.

But then, while I got so lonely and so small, he did so well. He kept telling me I was the reason for all the negative things in his life, and still, I wanted to stay, so I left my book in a closed folder on my hard drive, thinking it probably wasn't very good anyway.

I lived with that book about being lonely in love for three years, but a few months ago I was set free. Not because that's when he left me (he left long before that but still held on) but because that's when I let go and turned around. Completely. I just let it go, let it free fall from the ship while I faced the other way, into the sun, the light, the new. Now I live in a different country and I'm writing a book about the magical way a life can change in just a few months when you simply decide to let go. When you move on. When you turn around. When you quit caring about someone's opinion who doesn't care about yours.

I've collected a list of things he's done that are selfish. I started collecting it five years ago, planning to one day show him. One of those days when he calls me to tell me how happy he is, how well he's doing without wishing the same for me. At the end of one of those calls, I planned to one day tell him that he's not a big person. He is not a loving person. I planned to list the things he's done one by one then tell him I'm above that and I deserve more.

The childish things anger and pain make you do...

Maybe a year ago I would have kept the list, but I'm bigger now. He's not the one who needs to know that he was wrong—I am the one who needs to know that I was right.
I no longer need his approval.
That, is letting go.

Some days it all comes back to me, but deep inside I know I've moved on. I no longer need him to know all the 87 ways he's done me wrong.

I love my cursed heartaches and empty nights. They feel so crisp and special when I put them into words.

ABOUT THE AUTHOR

Charlotte Eriksson is a songwriter and author from Sweden, currently living somewhere in Europe, in between the city and the ocean. She left everything she had and knew as a teenager, and moved to England to create a life for herself that made her excited to wake up in the morning. Since then she has started her own artist collective *Broken Glass Records*, written five books (*Empty Roads & Broken Bottles; in search for The Great Perhaps, Another Vagabond Lost To Love, You're Doing Just Fine, Everything changed when I forgave myself* and *He loved me some days. I'm sure he did*) and released 9 EPs and 4 LPs under the artist name The Glass Child. Her writings have been published on sites like Thought Catalog, Bella Grace Magazine and Rebelle Society.

AUTHOR NOTE

As a small independent author, I write books for the pure fulfillment of connecting with souls out there, who might be like me. Who might recognize themselves in my story. If you have found any joy or comfort in my words, please don't be shy ... Say hi to me online, send me a photo of you and this book, tag me on instagram, or tell me about a memory you'll never forget. If you want to help me tell the world about my books and story, there is no better way to support an independent author than to leave a 5-star review on Amazon, Goodreads and/or Audible. Tell all your friends and family about it.

Share your favorite quote from the book on instagram, tumblr, twitter … Tag me so I can find you!

Here's to growth through loss. Here's to reinvention and transformation, over and over again.

Thank you for being you.

Love always,
Charlotte

I have four other books called:

Everything Changed When I Forgave Myself
You're Doing Just Fine
Another Vagabond Lost To Love
Empty Roads & Broken Bottles; in search for The Great Perhaps

You can read all about them on my website :
www.CharlotteEriksson.com
www.instagram.com/justaglasschild

There you will also find excerpts, quotes and photos from the books.

You can get signed copies of all my books, signed CDs, merch and other creations in my online store: www.CharlotteEriksson.com/shop

If you want to support me to keep creating music and write books, I'd like to invite you to join me on Patreon:
www.Patreon.com/TheGlassChild

Quick find …

Printed in Great Britain
by Amazon

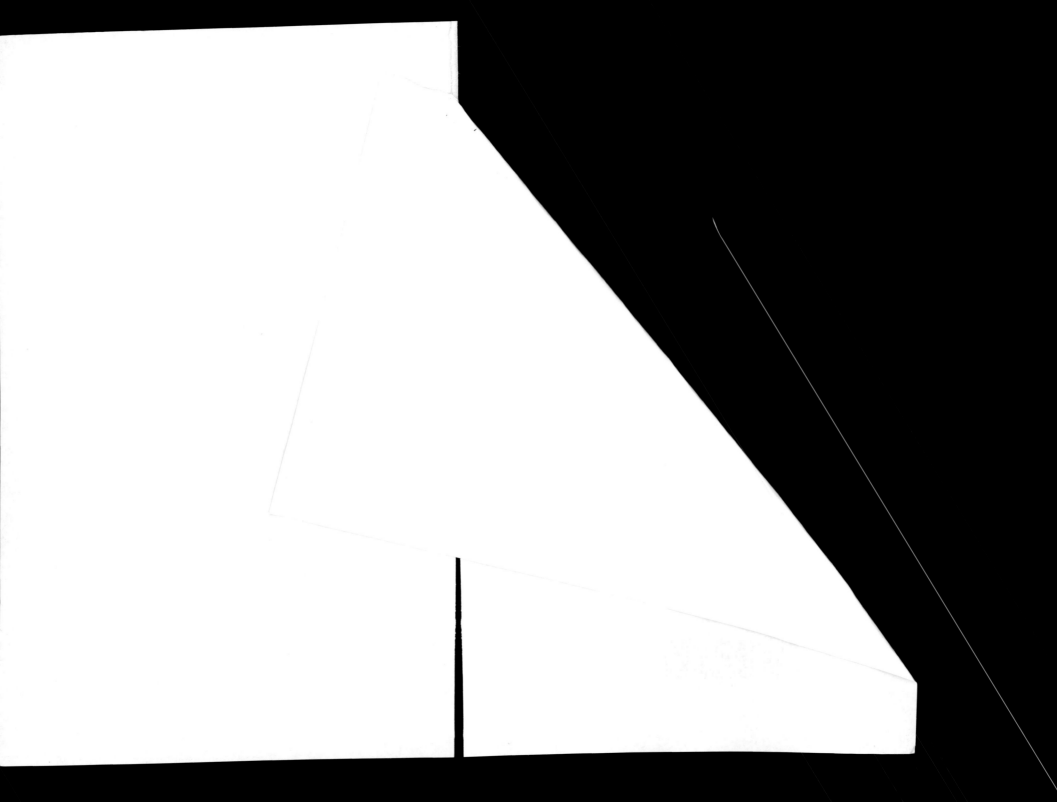